the post-black and post-white church

Becoming the Beloved Community in a Multi-Ethnic World

Efrem Smith

A Leadership Network Publication

JOSSEY-BASS
A Wiley Imprint
www.josseybass.com

Published by Jossey-Bass
A Wiley Imprint
One Montgomery Street, Suite 1200, San Francisco, CA 94104-4594—www.josseybass.com

Jossey-Bass books and products are available through most bookstores. To contact Jossey-Bass directly call our Customer Care Department within the U.S. at 800-956-7739, outside the U.S. at 317-572-3986, or fax 317-572-4002.

Wiley publishes in a variety of print and electronic formats and by print-on-demand. Some material included with standard print versions of this book may not be included in e-books or in print-on-demand. If this book refers to media such as a CD or DVD that is not included in the version you purchased, you may download this material at http://booksupport.wiley.com. For more information about Wiley products, visit www.wiley.com.

Scripture quotations taken from the New American Standard Bible®, Copyright © 1960, 1962, 1963, 1968, 1971, 1972, 1973, 1975, 1977, 1995 by The Lockman Foundation. Used by permission. (www.Lockman.org)

Library of Congress Cataloging-in-Publication Data

Smith, Efrem (Efrem D.), date
  The post-black and post-white church : becoming the beloved community in a multi-ethnic world / Efrem Smith. — 1st ed.
    p. cm. — (Jossey-Bass leadership network series ; 59)
  Includes index.
  ISBN 978-1-118-03658-7 (hardback); 978-1-118-26088-3 (ebk); 978-1-118-23606-2 (ebk); 978-1-118-22232-4 (ebk)
1. Church and minorities. 2. Social integration—Religious aspects—Christianity. 3. Reconciliation—Religious aspects—Christianity. 4. Multiculturalism—Religious aspects—Christianity I. Title.
  BV639.M56S65 2012
  277.3'083089--dc23

                                                                    2012012452

Printed in the United States of America
FIRST EDITION
HB Printing   10 9 8 7 6 5 4 3 2 1

leadership network titles

The Blogging Church: Sharing the Story of Your Church Through Blogs, Brian Bailey and Terry Storch

Church Turned Inside Out: A Guide for Designers, Refiners, and Re-Aligners, Linda Bergquist and Allan Karr

Leading from the Second Chair: Serving Your Church, Fulfilling Your Role, and Realizing Your Dreams, Mike Bonem and Roger Patterson

In Pursuit of Great AND Godly Leadership: Tapping the Wisdom of the World for the Kingdom of God, Mike Bonem

Hybrid Church: The Fusion of Intimacy and Impact, Dave Browning

The Way of Jesus: A Journey of Freedom for Pilgrims and Wanderers, Jonathan S. Campbell with Jennifer Campbell

Cracking Your Church's Culture Code: Seven Keys to Unleashing Vision and Inspiration, Samuel R. Chand

Leading the Team-Based Church: How Pastors and Church Staffs Can Grow Together into a Powerful Fellowship of Leaders, George Cladis

Organic Church: Growing Faith Where Life Happens, Neil Cole

Church 3.0: Upgrades for the Future of the Church, Neil Cole

Journeys to Significance: Charting a Leadership Course from the Life of Paul, Neil Cole

Church Transfusion: Changing Your Church Organically from the Inside Out, Neil Cole and Phil Helfer

Off-Road Disciplines: Spiritual Adventures of Missional Leaders, Earl Creps

Reverse Mentoring: How Young Leaders Can Transform the Church and Why We Should Let Them, Earl Creps

Building a Healthy Multi-Ethnic Church: Mandate, Commitments, and Practices of a Diverse Congregation, Mark DeYmaz

Leading Congregational Change Workbook, James H. Furr, Mike Bonem, and Jim Herrington

The Tangible Kingdom: Creating Incarnational Community, Hugh Halter and Matt Smay

Baby Boomers and Beyond: Tapping the Ministry Talents and Passions of Adults over Fifty, Amy Hanson

Leading Congregational Change: A Practical Guide for the Transformational Journey, Jim Herrington, Mike Bonem, and James H. Furr

The Leader's Journey: Accepting the Call to Personal and Congregational Transformation, Jim Herrington, Robert Creech, and Trisha Taylor

The Permanent Revolution: Apostolic Imagination and Practice for the 21st Century, Alan Hirsch and Tim Catchim

Whole Church: Leading from Fragmentation to Engagement, Mel Lawrenz

Culture Shift: Transforming Your Church from the Inside Out, Robert Lewis and Wayne Cordeiro, with Warren Bird

Church Unique: How Missional Leaders Cast Vision, Capture Culture, and Create Movement, Will Mancini

A New Kind of Christian: A Tale of Two Friends on a Spiritual Journey, Brian D. McLaren

The Story We Find Ourselves In: Further Adventures of a New Kind of Christian, Brian D. McLaren

Missional Communities: The Rise of the Post-Congregational Church, Reggie McNeal

Missional Renaissance: Changing the Scorecard for the Church, Reggie McNeal

Practicing Greatness: 7 Disciplines of Extraordinary Spiritual Leaders, Reggie McNeal

The Present Future: Six Tough Questions for the Church, Reggie McNeal

A Work of Heart: Understanding How God Shapes Spiritual Leaders, Reggie McNeal

The Millennium Matrix: Reclaiming the Past, Reframing the Future of the Church, M. Rex Miller

Your Church in Rhythm: The Forgotten Dimensions of Seasons and Cycles, Bruce B. Miller

Shaped by God's Heart: The Passion and Practices of Missional Churches, Milfred Minatrea

The Missional Leader: Equipping Your Church to Reach a Changing World, Alan J. Roxburgh and Fred Romanuk

Missional Map-Making: Skills for Leading in Times of Transition, Alan J. Roxburgh

Relational Intelligence: How Leaders Can Expand Their Influence Through a New Way of Being Smart, Steve Saccone

The Post-Black and Post-White Church: Becoming the Beloved Community in a Multi-Ethnic World, Efrem Smith

Viral Churches: Helping Church Planters Become Movement Makers, Ed Stetzer and Warren Bird

The Externally Focused Quest: Becoming the Best Church for the Community, Eric Swanson and Rick Rusaw

The Ascent of a Leader: How Ordinary Relationships Develop Extraordinary Character and Influence, Bill Thrall, Bruce McNicol, and Ken McElrath

Beyond Megachurch Myths: What We Can Learn from America's Largest Churches, Scott Thumma and Dave Travis

The Other 80 Percent: Turning Your Church's Spectators into Active Participants, Scott Thumma and Warren Bird

Better Together: Making Church Mergers Work, Jim Tomberlin and Warren Bird

The Elephant in the Boardroom: Speaking the Unspoken About Pastoral Transitions, Carolyn Weese and J. Russell Crabtree

contents

To the pastors who raised me: Art Erickson, Edward Berry Sr., Keith Johnson, Bart Campolo, and Gerald Joiner

about the jossey-bass leadership network series

Leadership Network's mission is to accelerate the impact of 100X leaders. These high-capacity leaders are like the hundredfold crop that comes from seed planted in good soil as Jesus described in Matthew 13:8.

Leadership Network

- Explores the "what's next?" of what could be
- Creates "aha!" environments for collaborative discovery
- Works with exceptional "positive deviants"
- Invests in the success of others through generous relationships
- Pursues big impact through measurable kingdom results
- Strives to model Jesus through all we do

Believing that meaningful conversations and strategic connections can change the world, we seek to help leaders navigate the future by exploring new ideas and finding application for each unique context. Through collaborative meetings and processes, leaders map future possibilities and challenge one another to action that accelerates fruitfulness and effectiveness. Leadership Network shares the learnings and inspiration with others through our books, concept papers, research reports, e-newsletters, podcasts, videos, and online experiences. This in turn generates a ripple effect of new conversations and further influence.

In 1996, Leadership Network established a partnership with Jossey-Bass, a Wiley Imprint, to develop a series of creative books that would provide thought leadership to innovators in church ministry. *Leadership Network publications present thoroughly researched and innovative concepts* from leading thinkers, practitioners, and pioneering churches.

To learn more about Leadership Network, go to www.leadnet.org.

foreword

The demographic changes occurring as we draw closer to the midpoint of the twenty-first century are prompting a mixture of reactions and responses. If the projections are accurate, by the early 2040s the United States will be a nation without a demographic majority. Whites will drop below 50 percent of the population. In the next ten to fifteen years this will happen for those under the age of eighteen years. It is already true for births in the United States. The 2008 election of Barack Obama as the nation's first Black president, after forty-three consecutive White male presidents, demonstrated that attitudes about race were shifting among a new generation of voters. Some declared that we had entered a post-racial era. Many of us had a growing optimism about the possibility for increasing the numbers of congregations that crossed the dividing lines of race, culture, class, gender, and the like. We even called for a movement of such congregations to serve as models of reconciliation for the broader society.

Yet we have discovered that racial divisions still loom large in the nation's life together. The euphoria of the Obama election and the apparent moment of national reconciliation have faded, now replaced for some by anxiety, fear, and anger as the racial demographics in the United States continue to become more and more diverse. I often wonder if our highly charged political discourse is the result of simmering discontent, just below the surface, about what it means to live in a nation where Whites are no longer in the majority. As I write, the outcry at the killing of a hoodie-wearing African-American teen has launched a national conversation about the continued reality of racial profiling in the lives of citizens of color. Also, this season of national discontent has caused some of us to reflect on the state of our movement for diverse congregations that model reconciliation. Have our attempts at developing reconciled congregations produced demographically diverse Sunday celebrations but offered limited attention to racialized lives and institutional structures?

The Post-Black and Post-White Church arrives at a time when the United States is rediscovering that the effects of its history of racial division are still deeply embedded in the psyches of its people and in the systems that sustain and maintain the country's institutions. Efrem Smith's urgent call for a beloved community rings forth as so many multi-ethnic congregations are struggling to live out the demands of an authentic biblically reconciled fellowship. So this book is very timely!

Efrem Smith is uniquely qualified to write this book. I have known Efrem for nearly twenty-five years. He has lived his life in both African-American and White contexts. He is deeply rooted in his own African-American historical and cultural context yet he easily interacts in White communities. Crossing racial and cultural divides in ways that celebrate difference and promote unity has been his life work. This book shares what he has learned from many years of reconciliation work and, in particular, as the founding pastor of Sanctuary Covenant Church—a multi-ethnic congregation I have observed closely since its beginning. Efrem Smith embodies his vision of the church moving toward a post-Black and post-White ethic.

I must admit I was at first a bit troubled by the terms "post-Black" and "post-White" as applied to the church. The idea of leaving a part of our identity behind did not resonate with me. But as I read this book I discovered that this is not what was meant by Smith. In fact, I found much to be encouraged by. First, the book calls for the formation of multi-ethnic congregations. These congregations should be post-Black and post-White in the sense that they are representative of the next step beyond our long history of racially divided churches in the United States. Therefore, post-Black means that multiethnic congregations must hold on to the most important elements and gifts of the African-American church. To be post-White means that multi-ethnic congregations must let go of the socially constructed Whiteness that so permeates the dominant culture of the United States and reclaim remnants of European cultures that were discarded in the U.S. melting pot project. When this process occurs, Smith argues, congregations will become reconciled, multi-ethnic, and missional. Echoing Martin Luther King Jr., his subtitle envisions the role of these churches—*Becoming the Beloved Community in a Multi-Ethnic World*.

I deeply appreciate the honesty and transparency with which Efrem Smith shares his insights and stories. He writes as a fellow traveler on the journey. He notes his weaknesses and shortcomings as opportunities for all of us to learn how to become stronger leaders. I congratulate Efrem Smith on this fine work that inspires us to envision a more reconciled future and compels us to do the hard work to get closer to becoming the beloved community.

Curtiss Paul DeYoung
Professor of Reconciliation Studies
Bethel University, St. Paul, MN

introduction: enter the sanctuary

L et me take you to church for a moment. This is not a typical church in the United States. Rather, the Sanctuary Covenant Church is a multi-ethnic and missional church located in North Minneapolis, Minnesota.

It's the beginning of spring in Minnesota (which means there could still be a chance for a blizzard to come on the scene at any time), and on this particular Sunday morning, an experience of corporate worship is about to begin that has been focused for the past seven weeks on racial reconciliation and unity. The series is called "Community."

This series is tied to a broader campaign that the church has been focused on all year: Vision for the City. The goal of the campaign was to break down the purpose statement of the church—"To change the face of the church in America by reconciling the people of the city to God and one another"—in a way that would provide applications for increasing its engagement in the community of North Minneapolis and strengthen the church as a multi-ethnic congregation.

All of the sermons this year lift up important elements intended to provide practical ways for living out the church's purpose. The intended immediate outcome is that the church might be more fruitful in terms of transforming the lives of community residents. The hope is that by focusing on reconciliation, the church members and regular attendees will collectively own the core values, purpose, and vision of the church. The Vision for the City campaign includes not only what goes on through the experience of corporate worship on Sunday morning but also an all-church Bible study on racial reconciliation and multi-ethnic fellowship gatherings during the week. The hope is that the gatherings will play a role in the development of multi-ethnic community groups within the church, which are this church's version of small groups ministry (groups of ten to twenty people who meet outside of the Sunday morning worship and focus on spiritual growth and development).

This Sunday morning, the worship leader is an African-American woman who uses music and other forms of creative arts to encourage the congregation to be involved in the experience of worship from the very beginning. This time also sets up the general theme for this particular worship service, and later, the senior pastor delivers a sermon around this theme. She begins with an opening prayer and then leads a time of praise and worship that includes the sounds of hip-hop, soul, rock, and urban gospel. The Praise and Worship Band moves rhythmically, sounding first like Earth, Wind, and Fire, a rhythm and blues music group; then Kirk Franklin, an urban contemporary gospel artist; and then the David Crowder Band, a six-piece modern Christian band. A multi-ethnic group of singers and two hip-hop emcees, also known as rappers, provide the opportunity to worship God through song in various styles. Their placement on the worship team is intended to reach both a multi-ethnic congregation and members of the surrounding community who are lured in by the sound moving through the neighborhood, flyers that are put in barbershops and hair salons, and word of mouth. Although these talented musicians have the ability to play worship songs in a diversity of genres, the sound most often heard is a soulful and urban one. This is why some call the worship leader the "Patti LaBelle of the Sanctuary Covenant Church." Younger worshippers of the hip-hop generation call her the "Mary J. Blige of worship." In fact, she spans generations: she can easily go from a 1970s soul singer, to a hip-hop queen, and then to a contemporary Christian music worship leader. She invites people into the worship by calling the congregation to "get your hands in the air; get your hands in the air right now. If you know what's going down, and Christ wears the crown, get your hands in the air right now!"

As powerful a vocalist as this worship leader is, she does more than entertain us. Her charismatic, contagious, and passionate personality is so tied into the anointing that is on her that it invites the congregation into energetic worship. Nevertheless, it's hard not to notice how talented she is. She is contemporary in style but also has the gospel roots of the Black church within her, a quality of no small importance when leading a multi-ethnic congregation of a thousand people in praise and worship. She provides a welcoming smile, shares her joys and pains, makes everyone laugh, and even raps a bit. She brings a kind of vulnerability to her dancing, shouting, and calling us to "come on and give God some praise up in here!"

The worship band features a leader, who is multi-ethnic and has played with such R&B artists as Alexander O'Neil, Janet Jackson, and Paula Abdul. He now uses his music gifts for ministry in the church to reach others who love an urban sound but have yet to know Christ as their Lord and Savior. Most Sundays the worship band consists of a lead guitar, a bass guitar, a drummer, two keyboards, percussion, and occasionally a horn section. This is why I compared the band's sound at times to Earth, Wind, and Fire.

The worship and band leaders work together using their gifts to lead the congregation through their own versions of "Awesome God," "Breath," and "What a Friend We Have in Jesus." The diverse praise and worship includes hymns, Black church gospel standards, and contemporary praise and worship, but they become a unified sound through "putting the spice on it." This means adding a hip-hop, rhythm-and-blues style to the service.

During the time of praise and worship, you probably find that these different genres of worship, blended into an urban sound, have drawn you deeply in. In fact, African-American urban music has a universal sound that has brought people of many cultures and ethnicities together in America. Jazz, the Motown sound, and now hip-hop have influenced and brought people together across races in a way that other music styles have not.

As you look around at the congregation, you notice that about half the worshippers are White in this service, which can be characterized as hip-hop, neosoul, and urban gospel in style. This reality underscores the influence of African-American and urban music and how it has become what I refer to as post-Black music: the music of Black folks originally that has emerged as the music of America and, in fact, the rest of the world. And there is no question that within this experience of worship, the music is being taken in and owned by a multicultural audience, which is presenting this urban worship style as a gift to God. Through this style of praise and worship, the congregation has grown in just over four years into an intergenerational and multi-ethnic community of a thousand people, with a membership of close to four hundred.

The community in this sanctuary is more than multi-ethnic; it is also intergenerational. The children do not go to Sunday school until after the service. And the contemporary and relevant approach draws older young people to the experience of corporate worship.

You may also notice as you look around that not everyone is clapping, dancing, or jumping up and down. Some are simply standing or sitting, but nevertheless taking it all in. This suggests that not everyone at the Sanctuary is here for the praise and worship style. During the meet-and-greet time after the service, you may find some worshippers who admit that the music is not really their personal taste. For them, the atmosphere that models a sneak preview of heaven on earth draws them in and moves to something beyond just a tolerance of this church's praise and worship style.

There is a Spirit-led, organic "something" that takes place at the Sanctuary Covenant Church that is difficult to put words to, but if we are willing to live in this "something," it will point us on a larger scale to the future of the church in the United States and beyond. Some are drawn to the Sanctuary Sunday after Sunday because of something unique within the multi-ethnic church. There is sense of what Dr. Martin Luther King Jr. called "the beloved community." This kind of community, which dares to be post-Black and post-White, is a multi-ethnic and missional church. The people who are drawn to this kind of worship believe that this is the church that God desires. Note that throughout this book, I use *post-Black* and *post-White* to refer to an experience that is beyond a racially segregated one. Historically, and even in some cases today, the most visible sign of segregation is Black and White.

The meet-and-greet time following the praise and worship is important because it assists each week in moving people from simply being in a diverse crowd to building an authentic multi-ethnic community. Before the sermon, members of the reconciliation design team present a dramatic spoken-word piece entitled, "Where I'm From." The piece is presented by a multi-ethnic group of women and men who tell the unique stories of their upbringing, faith journey, and personal take on the world around them. They end by asking in unison, "Where are you from?" They proclaim together that it is possible to live in a Christ-centered and reconciling community that equips and empowers people to advance the kingdom of God and celebrate diversity. By discovering that advancing the kingdom of God and ethnic diversity is biblical, we are able to celebrate various ethnicities, cultures, and languages as members of God's family.

As senior pastor of the Sanctuary, I preach a sermon after the spoken-word piece entitled "Reconciliation and Worship," which I end with an altar call.[1] Many people come up to the altar that day, some for prayer and others to accept Jesus Christ as their Lord and Savior. As I look at people of all different backgrounds committing to becoming ambassadors of reconciliation and praying in front of the stage in this school auditorium, I'm overwhelmed by this diverse and beautiful picture.

Stay with me for moment, and maybe you can feel what I am. This is the church as it should be: no dividing walls and a glimpse of heaven. I'm awed, speechless, frozen, warm, and for a moment even removed from the fact that I'm the senior pastor. I look up at the larger group of multi-ethnic people and ask myself, *How did this happen?* followed by, *Thank you, Lord, for the opportunity to be a part of this!*

After worship, people are now gathered in what is called the Fellowship Café. I'm watching this diverse group of people eating, laughing, chasing after small children, and making plans to connect later in the week. I find myself, as always, feeling blessed to be part of this church.

This praise and worship experience is something special and out of the norm for church in America. The Sanctuary Covenant Church is not the only multi-ethnic church in the United States, but it doesn't represent the majority of churches in America. In fact, the most visible picture of the church in the United States is one divided by race. I grew up for the most part seeing two kinds of churches, the Black church and the White church, and I believed that this was normal. Yet the neighborhood I grew up in and the schools I attended were multi-ethnic, so I did wonder why there were these separate churches. Even at a young age, I yearned to be part of a church that went beyond the church of Black and White. This is why I call the Sanctuary a post-Black, post-White church. It represents something beyond the church segregated by race by bringing people together to provide a sneak preview of heaven.

In fact, in the United States, society has accepted the homogeneous and segregated church as the normal church. I think about this and grieve because I want the norm of the church in America to be one that lives in the tension and victory of the first church in the book of Acts and the picture of heaven that we see in Revelation 7:9: "After these things I looked, and behold a great multitude, which no one could count, from every nation and all tribes and peoples and tongues, standing before the throne and before the Lamb" (Revelation 7:9).[2] To become a multi-ethnic church like the Sanctuary Covenant Church within a society that is very much racialized is no easy task. It takes much work to develop an intentionally multi-ethnic board and staff made up of African-Americans, Asian-Americans, and European-Americans.[3] The weekly attendance by ethnicity at the time of my departure from the Sanctuary Covenant Church in 2010 to serve as a regional superintendent within the Evangelical Covenant church was about 55 percent European-American, 35 percent African-American, and the rest Latino and Asian. Many who attended Sunday morning worship commented, "This is what church is supposed to look like."

As I departed this church, a movement had already risen from this relatively young church. The Sanctuary Covenant Church has already participated in supporting the launching of other multi-ethnic and missional churches: Sanctuary Columbus in Columbus, Ohio, led by Richard Johnson; Blue Oaks Covenant Church in Brooklyn Park, Minnesota, led by Nicole Bullock; and Urban Jerusalem, a multi-ethnic and hip-hop church led by Stacey Jones, also in North Minneapolis. Serving now in a regional ministry position, I seek to continue in the development of intentionally multi-ethnic and missional churches. But it all began with the planting of a church in Minneapolis.

As an African-American male in my forties, I often wonder how I came to pastor this amazing church full of the signs and wonders of God while also living in the spiritual warfare of the racialized matrix of the United States. The Sanctuary is a unique church in a society that is still trapped in the historic framework of the church in Black and White. It was started to create a movement that would help make the multi-ethnic and missional church the norm for church in this country. A team of Christian sociologists and reconciliation studies leaders has defined a multiracial congregation as one "in which no one racial group accounts for 80 percent or more of the membership."[4] In other words, a multiracial church is one with only 20 percent diversity. You would think that if this is all it takes for a congregation to be called multi-ethnic, that these churches would be common across the country. This is not the case. There has been no increase in the creation of what I call "beloved churches and communities," which can serve as visible manifestations of a post-Black, post-White church movement. We need them. These types of churches could lead to the realization of the beloved community, a glimpse of the kingdom of God right here and right now. As Curtiss DeYoung and his colleagues say, "The twenty-first century must be the century of the multiracial congregations."[5] My hope is to inspire many to say yes to this call.

reconciling, multi-ethnic, and missional

When the Sanctuary Covenant Church was planted in 2003, there was an intentional plan to develop a core team, a leadership structure, a worship experience, and eventually a staff that was culturally diverse. As the church planter, I began this journey with a heart and vision for a church that would be a kingdom church and a reconciling community. Although I grew up in the Black church, I was inspired by the stories of John Perkins and his ministry of reconciliation and Martin Luther King Jr.'s vision of the beloved community, a term he used to cast a vision of racial equality, justice, and reconciliation. Through this lens, I was able to imagine the church in a new way. I deal with this journey and these influences throughout this book.

By "kingdom church," I mean one that is willing to move away from one primarily shaped by race. I use "matrix of race" to refer to the ways in which we remain trapped by race, which continues to have more power than we like to admit. In many circles, even bringing up the issue of race causes fear, tension, and defensiveness. And

1

our being trapped in the matrix is also revealed through how natural it seems to be with people who look and act like us and how challenging it is to build authentic relationships and community with people who are different. This seems particularly challenging in the church, and that is why we are in need of a different church—one that is a picture of the kingdom proclaimed by and embodied in Jesus Christ. This kingdom is Christ centered and multi-ethnic because Jesus walked the earth as the Messiah, the Son of God, and was, as Curtiss DeYoung says "an Afro-Asiatic Jew."[1] The church of the kingdom of God transcends race, yet recognizes the beauty of ethnic diversity because this diversity existed in Jesus, who is the embodiment of the kingdom.

I speak of the post-Black, post-White church as a reconciling community because Jesus is also the ultimate reconciler. Consider this passage from 2 Corinthians (5:18–19): "Now all these things are from God, who reconciled us to Himself through Christ, and gave us the ministry of reconciliation, namely that God was in Christ reconciling the world to Himself, not counting their trespasses against them, and He has committed to us the word of reconciliation."

Jesus reconciles us to God through his death and resurrection. We are freed from the penalty of sin, which is death, through Jesus. This reconciling work not only brings us into an intimate and right relationship with God but also empowers us through the Holy Spirit to experience the right relationship with each other.

A post-Black, post-White church unplugs us from the sinful and unbiblical race matrix (in fact, there is nothing about race in the Bible, a topic I turn to in Chapter Three) of Black and White and liberates us to live in an otherworldly, countercultural kingdom church and reconciling community. It's what Dave Gibbons, senior pastor of New Song Church, a multi-ethnic church in Southern California, refers to as "third culture." Third culture is the creation of kingdom culture on earth—the beloved community. It is within

believers from all nations
Rev

the prayer that Jesus taught the original disciples to pray: "The Kingdom to come and God's will to be done on earth as it is in heaven" (Matthew 6:10). Gibbons describes third culture as a biblical mandate for the church to make disciples within this multicultural reality. This ought to be the first reason for the development of the post-Black, post-White church. We pursue a multi-ethnic church because we are passionate about the lost being found in a diverse surrounding demographic. Some shun the multi-ethnic church because they see it as a mark of political correctness. But ultimately, as Pastor Mark DeYmaz points out, "The pursuit of the multi-ethnic local church is in my view, not optional. It is biblically mandated for all who aspire to lead local congregations of faith."[2]

We ought to pursue this kind of church because it represents a church after God's own heart and because as we live in it, we receive a deeper understanding of what it means to be children of God and the bride of Christ. This is why both the terms post-Black, post-White church and beloved community are so important.

The Racial Divide

There are many ethnic forms of church in the United States: Asian, Hispanic, and first-generation African immigrant churches. And certainly these types of ethnic-specific churches move us beyond the church in Black and White as we have known it. But the most visible pictures of the church in the United States are the White church and the Black church. The White church isn't referred to as "White" most of the time because it is seen as "the church." That is, the White church is the American church, the average church, and almost all research on churches is based on it.

The Black church reflects the historic divide between Black and White people in this country: it is a forced church that emerged out of slavery. Both the White and the Black church in the United States are tied deeply to the story of slavery, Jim Crow segregation, the civil rights movement, and even more contemporary stories with race implications, such as Rodney King, Hurricane Katrina, and the presidential election of Barack Obama.

When sociologists want to provide evidence that the racial divide remains, they often look to the church for their facts. In fact, Martin Luther King Jr. called the church "the most segregated major institution in America." He called Sunday morning, when the congregation rises to sing "In Christ There Is No East or West," the "most segregated hour of America, and . . . Sunday school is the most segregated school of the week."[3] The question today is, How much has really changed since King spoke? I am an evangelical, and with this comes a belief in the authority and centrality of scripture. With this in mind, how can the evangelical church not see the impact that race has had on it? I don't believe that the issue ultimately is that the evangelical church doesn't see it; it does see it, but it doesn't know what to do about it. Mainline churches struggle with this issue as well even though their theology is more consistent with multiculturalism. Yet their belief that their theology is progressive around issues of multiculturalism causes them not to see their own structural issues of race at times. Still, not knowing what to do about it shouldn't keep us from confessing the sin of our participation in the trap and desiring something closer to God's heart for the church.

In fact, the matrix of race in this country is changing. In 2008 history was made with the election of the first African-American president. Some used this historic moment to point to the development of an emerging postracial reality that is global. Religious scholar Phillip Jenkins believes that the future of the church has moved beyond the United States and Europe to Africa and South America. He writes, "Over the past century . . . the center of gravity in the Christian world has shifted inexorably southward, to Africa, Asia, and Latin America. . . . Christianity should enjoy a worldwide boom in the new century, but the vast majority of believers will be neither white nor European, nor Euro-American."[4]

So this reality means that the church in the United States must change—not primarily for social reasons but for biblical reasons. You would be hard-pressed to find scripture to justify the social structure of race or the racially divided church.

The Beloved Community

The multi-ethnic and missional church points us to a church where God's love rescues people from the matrix and sin of racial division and delivers us into the reconciling spirit of the beloved community. These churches alone may not totally eradicate or dismantle our race-based society, but they will provide the alternative that many of us hunger for. The multi-ethnic and missional church as a Christ-centered community becomes the beloved community that Martin Luther King Jr. spoke of. It indeed becomes the beloved church that forges the beloved community in the world.[5] This is true kingdom advancement.

In the first-century church, kingdom advancement was not separated into Jewish and Gentile, and today it cannot be separated from issues of race and class within a multicultural society. The common denominator here is kingdom advancement. This is the missional side of the multi-ethnic church. The church is God's primary vehicle for fulfilling his mission in the world.

The beloved community gives us a more biblically based way to talk about evangelism, discipleship, and mission in this changing world. The term *beloved* shows up often in the writings of John in the New Testament in his gospel writing and his letters. As one of the original followers of Christ, John saw himself as the dearly loved of God. He seemed to find identity in this state of belovedness, and beloved is at the core of God's great love for us. God looked beyond our sins and offered his Son, Jesus, to die on the cross in order that we might come into the full realization of being the beloved children of God. John wrote, "See how great a love the Father has bestowed upon us, that we should be called children of God; and such we are. For this reason the world does not know us, because it did not know him. Beloved, we are children of God, and it has not appeared as yet what we shall be. We know that, when He appears, we shall be like Him, because we shall see Him just as He is" (1 John 3:1–2).

Belovedness is also a reconciling force at the core of a multi-ethnic and missional church. God's love for us flows through us that we might live in community and unity outside the race structures of this world and express that love for one another and the world. Again we turn to John: "Beloved let us love one another, for love is from God; and everyone who loves is born of God. The one who does not love does not know God, for God is love. By this the love of God was manifested in us, that God sent His only begotten Son into the world so that we might live through Him" (1 John 4:7–9).

"Beloved" is what connects us in an intimate relationship with Christ, relationships with one another in the body of Christ, and our ability to advance the kingdom of God. We must be willing to honestly unpack what keeps us from loving one another. It may be easier to plant, grow, and sustain a homogeneous church in Black or White, but it's unbiblical. And even though it's harder to plant, grow, and sustain a multi-ethnic and beloved church, it's a biblical mandate. As the Gospel of Matthew comes to a conclusion, the resurrected Jesus set forth the Great Commission: he called his followers to go beyond just reaching their own Jewish people, to making disciples of all nations (Matthew 28:19). The homogeneous church model narrows both the Great Commission and the gospel.

The post-Black, post-White church should frame the future of the church in the United States. I have been a part of and listened to too many discussions about the postmodern church that are limited by White church theology, philosophy, and practice. Many of the so-called emerging, missional, and monastic discussions, conferences, books, and blogs are mainly about the current state and future of the White church. Similarly, the megachurch in the United States is accepted and marketed as the best practice model for church development, planting, and revitalization. But many of these megachurches are also stuck in the matrix of Black and White. Yet neither our current reality nor the future is White. We need to include or replace the models, language, and approaches with post-Black, post-White theology and practice because they will lead to the development of kingdom churches.

The Church's Struggle with Race

The good news is that some of the most respected megachurch leaders are now lifting up the importance and the biblical mandate for multi-ethnic and missional churches. One such leader is Bill Hybels, senior pastor of Willow Creek Church and president of the Willow Creek Association of Churches. Over the past few years at the Leadership Summit Conference, he has been transparent about Willow Creek's intentional journey to be more missional through a focus on deep discipleship and by becoming a multi-ethnic church. We can only hope that more megachurches will move in this direction.

The discussion on multi-ethnic churches is the most important one that those concerned about the church in post-Christendom should be having. But many of these discussions are limited by not acknowledging that the theological constructs and frameworks being used are stuck in Whiteness and more rooted in philosophy than theology. I don't put the blame totally on European-Americans because at least they're having the discussion. Most times when I bring up this issue with European-American pastors and ministry leaders, they readily acknowledge the problem of being stuck in White church ideologies and structures. I've also had some fruitful discussions with members of the emergent movement, missional church movements, and leaders of denominations about the importance of multi-ethnic church and ministry development in today's multicultural reality.

Sometimes leaders within the Black church are more resistant to this kind of multi-ethnic and biblical discussion. As the world is becoming more and more multi-ethnic and multicultural, a significant portion of the Black church seems stuck in survival mode instead of being the innovative force behind a multi-ethnic and missional church. This may be because race is still a large a factor in our society. Many argue that the Black church is still needed—not because the White church is not welcoming to other ethnicities but because of a power dynamic that promotes assimilation. The unspoken question is, "What will African-Americans lose by being in a multi-ethnic community, specifically with European-Americans?" Sociologist Korie Edwards addresses this issue of power dynamics within what she calls interracial churches:

> In short, I propose that interracial churches work, that is, remain racially integrated, to the extent that they are first comfortable places for whites to attend. This is not to suggest, of course, that the congregational life of interracial churches only represents the interests and preferences of whites. Indeed, these churches need to also appeal to the racial minorities in their religious communities. Nevertheless, whiteness plays a critical role in how interracial churches are organized, ultimately producing churches that reflect a congregational life more commonly seen in white churches than in others.[6]

With this in mind, why would African-American leaders want to abandon the Black church for a multi-ethnic church that could eventually become a church mainly catering to Whites? A number of questions have to be answered: Can there be a fruitful focus on issues specifically facing African-Americans and the African-American community within an interracial church? When European-Americans enter an interracial church, does it cause the other congregants to assimilate into Whiteness and lose their distinctive racial or ethnic characteristics, values, and gifts? These are important questions that have to be answered, which is why a discussion on a post-Black, post-White church is necessary. Within these discussions, we can't pretend we can have color-blind visions for a different kind of church. We have to deal with the issues of Blackness and Whiteness that drive why the church looks the way it does. This is why I choose to use the term multi-ethnic and not interracial. This book deals primarily with the issue of finding identity in race, which is not of God. Multi-ethnicity is a more biblical and God-honoring way of being a Christ-centered and reconciling community than race. At the same time, we cannot ignore the daily implications of race in our society.

I realize that the church is already much more than Black and White, but it is still struggling to break out of the matrix of race, which is very much rooted in the historic Black and White conflict. There are churches that I've attended that are predominantly Asian or Hispanic, but with the exception of the language difference in the first-generation churches, they tend to take on Black or White characteristics, and most of the time, it's White characteristics. I sat in a worship recently at a second- and third-generation Asian church, and when I closed my eyes, the praise and worship sounded as if I was in a contemporary White worship service. Clearly other ethnic churches in the United States are stuck in this race matrix of Black and White, and maybe more than we'd like to admit. These cases of ethnic churches functioning as White churches go back to my point of the White church in America being considered the "normal church." The question then becomes, What is going on in society that causes some second- and third-generation ethnic groups to lose their sense of a unique cultural style of worship practice that could in turn be a blessing to other ethnicities?

The church must recognize that this matrix exists, unplug from it, and become a truly reconciling and kingdom-building force. This will not happen if we stay in denial about how much the race matrix is influencing the church. To a degree, in fact, race has a larger influence on the church than the Bible does.

In order to take advantage of the kingdom-advancing opportunities before us, we must plant and develop post-Black, post-White churches. The question then becomes, What does this look like? That what's this book is all about.

What This Book Is About

This book begins with a multi-ethnic and missional church planting and revitalization movement that is intentional about doing the hard work of developing post-Black, post-White churches. I realize that this is not the first book written on the development of multi-ethnic and missional churches. What may be unique about this one is that it combines multi-ethnic and missional.

Mark DeYmaz has laid the foundation for the development of multi-ethnic churches. He is the lead pastor of an intentionally multi-ethnic church in central Arkansas and the leader of a movement, the Mosaix Network, to develop more multi-ethnic churches. He locates the biblical mandate for the multi-ethnic church in John 17 when Jesus prays to the Father that his followers will remain unified as he prepares to go to the cross. He is thinking about how his disciples will be about kingdom-advancing work when he is no longer with them. DeYmaz presents the multi-ethnic church as a vehicle through which unity can be realized by the followers of Christ. This prayer provided a communal framework for Christ's Jewish and Gentile followers to live in unity. Within Acts, we see the transformation of Peter in a second conversion experience that leads him to the house of a Gentile named Cornelius. We see the diverse multi-ethnic leadership in the church at Antioch as well. DeYmaz concludes this biblical case by sharing the words of Paul to the Ephesians. Paul also deals with the local church of the first century as multi-ethnic, reconciling, and bringing unity between Jew and Gentile.

In many ways, I hope to build on the work that DeYmaz has done. I also believe that by connecting multi-ethnic with missional, this book is providing both a biblical and holistic model of church development, planting, and revitalization. I would say that I'm combining the writing of DeYmaz with that of John Perkins, one of the founders of the Christian Community Development Association and a heroic Christian leader for reconciliation in Mississippi. Perkins's writings around the principles of reconciliation, relocation, and redistribution planted the seeds in me that grew into a passion for the missional church. I first read Perkins's book *With Justice for All* as a teenager about a year after I became a Christian. I know now that his writings and preaching played a significant role in my initial theological development and my burden for a church beyond Black and White. Through Perkins, I discovered that the missional church is about the church being a vehicle of kingdom justice. Perkins captures that idea well:

I believe that justice for all can become a reality in America. Government alone though, however good, can never bring justice. I am convinced that the promise which our nation's laws alone have been powerless to fulfill can only be fulfilled in one way—through the power of the gospel of Jesus Christ. Yes, the gospel has this power. I know, for I have seen it bring hope to the hopeless; I have seen it empower the powerless to break the chains of oppression. I am persuaded that the Church, as a steward of this gospel, holds the key to justice in our society. Either justice will come through us or it will not come at all.[7]

I believe that Perkins is an overlooked voice when it comes to understanding the missional church. He is mostly seen as a voice for reconciliation, which he is. He is also seen by many as a voice for Christian community development, which he is. But he is also a pioneering voice for the multi-ethnic and missional church.

Perkins's missional strategy was centered around relocation, reconciliation, and redistribution. The relocation part of this strategy is about being among the lost and hurting of the world. This is what God did over two thousand years ago: he came from the heavenly realm and relocated to this broken and fallen world as the Son of God and God incarnate, both at the same time. The missional church is positioned among those in need of a savior. But we must remember that this Savior came to save the lost and to set us free as well. Jesus began his public ministry by speaking these words: "The Spirit of the LORD is upon Me because He anointed Me to preach the Gospel to the poor. He has sent me to proclaim release to the captives and recovery to the blind, to set free those who are downtrodden, to proclaim the favorable year of the Lord" (Luke 4:18–19). He then put those words into action: he forgave sins, gave mobility to the paralyzed, gave sight to the blind, and removed evil spirits. He did all of this and more as he showed us the holistic gospel. This is what Perkins is getting at in his missional strategy.

In the reconciliation part of his theology, Perkins points to the work of Jesus as he walked the earth among us, leading to his death and resurrection, as reconciling work. We are both reconciled to God through Christ Jesus and made ambassadors of reconciliation that we might have right relationships with one another. Perkins makes his case for the post-Black, post-White church here. In the 1960s and 1970s, he was questioning how the church can represent the great reconciler Jesus and not deal with race, the great dividing line during that time. This led him to plant a post-Black, post-White church:

> To carve out of the heart of Jackson, Mississippi, a community of believers reconciled to God and to each other—that was our dream; to bring together a fellowship of blacks and whites, rich and poor, who would live together, worship together and reach out together as the people of God. We believed that if we would faithfully be the people of God in our neighborhood, we could make a positive difference in the lives of people enslaved by poverty and racism.[8]

The post-Black, post-White church is a reconciling church that answers the call to justice, which is part of a holistic approach to the whole gospel. I believe this is where all missional church discussions should begin today. How is the church including kingdom justice in its approach to evangelism and outreach?

The combination of the biblical mandate for the multi-ethnic church presented by DeYmaz and the biblical framework for the missional church from Perkins provides part of the foundation for the post-Black, post-White church. Perkins's work was burning deep in my soul when I had the opportunity to plant the Sanctuary Covenant Church. He inspired a vision within me for a church in Minneapolis, where I grew up. DeYmaz provided similar inspiration for me in my role now as superintendent of the Pacific Southwest Conference of the Evangelical Covenant church. This relatively new leadership opportunity allows me to serve with a team to lead a movement of multi-ethnic and missional church development in California, Arizona, Hawaii, Nevada, and Utah.

This book provides biblical foundations, personal stories, church models, challenges, and encouragement for the planting of and the revitalization toward multi-ethnic and missional churches. Advancing the kingdom of God in the global and multi-ethnic realities that surround us is not about taking the easy road. And to be honest, if we look at the state of the majority of churches in the United States, that easy road really isn't getting us very far. The majority of churches in our country have fewer than one hundred people in the congregation, and many are dying. It's time to be intentional by developing post-Black, post-White churches that eventually become beloved communities of transformation in an increasingly multi-ethnic world. This will take a new discussion about the state of the church, as well as its vision, purpose, and core values. My hope is that the multi-ethnic church will become the norm of the church in America and beyond. The chapters that follow offer this hope.

2

moving the church beyond crisis, captivity, and comfort

The book of Jeremiah in the Old Testament is the story of the calling and challenge of a prophet sent to give an unpopular yet needed word to the people of God. The people of God were in captivity, and they had rejected the true God for false gods. God called Jeremiah to be a prophet when he was only a teenager, and over the course of more than forty years, he warned the people that their deliverance was connected to changing their ways. During this time, many of the other prophets were saying that things would be okay and that Jeremiah was a false prophet, so Jeremiah carried the heavy burden of convincing the people that things were not okay.

For those of us calling for the church in the United States to be more multi-ethnic and missional, this too seems at times like a heavy burden. There are many in the church of North America who believe the church is okay, as it in fact is for the most part. Nevertheless, there are some who are willing to be like Jeremiah, even though their voices are sometimes drowned out by a satisfaction with the homogeneous church model. They continue to push for a church that is more like that depicted in the book of Acts: made up of a multicultural community and therefore the first beloved community, which broke down the walls of social divisions of its day. They yearn for a church that reflects the kingdom of God. They want to be a part of a church that is a preview of where we will live eternally as God's beloved children. I am one of those voices. There are times when I have felt like Jeremiah. I am passionate about the multi-ethnic, missional, and reconciling church. But making the case for this kind of church can be hard, especially when there are so many who believe the church is fine the way it is.

A few years ago, I was at a large church planting conference. A popular megachurch pastor had just finished speaking in the afternoon's general session and was now backstage addressing a small group of church planters. After sharing a few words with us about the importance of church planting, there was an opportunity to ask questions, and I was the person to ask the last question. At the time, I had been leading a multi-ethnic and missional church for about five years, so I asked him what he thought about planting churches that would be intentionally multi-ethnic. His answer was like a punch in my gut: he said that he didn't believe in planting multi-ethnic churches and that people tend to be more comfortable going to church with people who look like them. He also said that planting a multi-ethnic church is like rolling a snowball uphill and reminded us that snowballs are meant to roll downhill in order to grow bigger and catch momentum. He was interested in growth and momentum, not the harder work of going uphill. After that, he began to joke about what a multicultural church plant would look like with people leading worship trying to sing country, hip-hop, and rock all at the same time. Then he looked at me and said, "Efrem, good for you to take on that challenge of planting multi-ethnic churches. I really respect that. But for the rest of us, we're going with the flow and the momentum." He then excused himself, more than likely headed to the next big conference he was scheduled to speak at. I stood in that room in silence for another twenty minutes feeling as if all the wind had been knocked out of me.

It's challenging to have a strong sense that the passion that burns inside you is biblical, Godly, and right yet seems unpopular with the majority of people talking about church planting, growth, and vitality. I praise God, though, that I've been able to meet others with the same burning passion for the post-Black, post-White church. There are others who also believe that all is not well with the church today, but they won't necessarily say that a multi-ethnic and missional the church is the solution to the problems in the church in America. They might talk about a missional church or becoming externally focused. But there aren't many who see multi-ethnic churches as the church of the New Testament. And there is little or no agreement that the church must be multi-ethnic in order to have evangelistic credibility in this ever-increasing multicultural reality. Still, I know and strongly believe that there can't be a truly missional conversation without a multi-ethnic component.

Why is it so hard to bring the need for a multi-ethnic and missional church to the forefront? One of the reasons lies in our current vision of and for the church. It is difficult for us as church leaders to see how the issue of race has blurred how we see the church. Pursuing the multi-ethnic and missional church begins with a sense of calling and then moves to our vision of church being aligned with God's vision. This is a strong statement: I am saying that the homogeneous church is not aligned with God's vision for the church. Race has a tremendous influence on how we see and develop churches, but it is unbiblical, as I have noted. I recognize and understand why we might take an ethnic-specific approach to ministry in some cases, perhaps with first-generation immigrant groups. And when it comes to evangelism in communities that are dominated by one ethnic group, developing a homogeneous approach makes sense. But thinking that homogeneous churches in communities that are multi-ethnic and multicultural is okay is a problem of vision. Calling and vision must be connected to each other and aligned with God. God calls Jeremiah and then aligns his vision: "Now the word of the Lord came to me saying, Before I formed you in the womb I knew you, And before you were born I consecrated you; I have appointed you a prophet to the nations" (Jeremiah 1:4–5).

How My Vision Became Aligned with God's Vision

I became a Christian when I was in high school through an outreach event, the Soul Liberation Festival, put on by a United Methodist church in my neighborhood. It was a large revival meeting of sorts and took place in the church parking lot. Each night there was a multi-ethnic choir that sang, followed by a preacher like Tony Campolo, John Perkins, or Joni Erickson Tada. I happened to be riding my bike past this event one night and was so struck by it that I came every night that week to hear more. I was moved by both the music and the preaching, and also drawn by the diversity of the event. This especially touched me because until that point, I knew the church only as Black or White. I was a member of a Black church and went every Sunday with my mother and grandmother. It was at this outdoor event, with its multi-ethnic diversity, that I was led to give my life to Christ.

I left the Soul Liberation Festival that first evening so excited. When my mother what had happened to me, she said to me, "This makes so much sense. When I was pregnant with you, my grandmother who had gone on to be with Jesus spoke to me in a dream one night. She said that the baby in my womb would be a preacher!" I must admit that this didn't really excite me. It made me very nervous; actually it made me scared.

It did make sense, though, because I later had regular dreams of standing in front of a diverse crowd and preaching the gospel. Could it be that like Jeremiah, I was set to be a part of the multi-ethnic and missional church before I was born? If a Methodist church in my neighborhood hadn't pursued being a multi-ethnic and missional church, would I have had this conversion experience and understood the purpose of God's call on my life? Because of this experience, I came to the realization that I was consecrated by God for a multi-ethnic ministry. On those summer evenings at the Methodist church, I had my vision of the church transformed. I no longer saw the church in Black and White. I dreamed of a church like what I experienced at the Soul Liberation Festival.

From the moment when I was in high school that I became a committed Christian, I knew there was something not quite right about the church, but I didn't feel qualified to do anything about it. I was like Jeremiah, who cried out, "Then I said, Alas Lord God! Behold, I don't know how to speak, Because I am a youth" (Jeremiah 1:6). I was only a teenager, but even as a noncredentialed, teenage Christian, I knew that God had a call on my life, just as he had for Jeremiah: "But the LORD said to me, Do not say, I am a youth, Because everywhere I send you, you shall go, And all that I command you, you shall speak" (Jeremiah 1:7).

I didn't start preaching as a teenager, but by my senior year in high school, I was singing in a multiracial singing group, Soul Purpose. I had grown up singing in the choir in the Black church, just as my grandmother and my mother had. Singing in Soul Purpose gave me the opportunity to travel to many places and experience the diversity of God's church. We sang in urban Black churches as well as White churches in small towns. Because of our diversity, we sang Black gospel, contemporary Christian, and southern gospel music. Though we were teenagers, I know we had an impact on the church because we were an ethnically diverse group.

But as much as I enjoyed singing in Soul Purpose, I began to struggle more and more with the segregated church. As we sang in a Black church on one weekend and then in a White church on the next weekend, I wondered why these separate churches couldn't be one church in some way. I was born in 1969, on the other side of the civil rights movement, and the church was the only segregated institution that I encountered in my life. This experience of being in a diverse singing group and yet singing in churches that weren't diverse allowed my vision to align with God's vision for the church.

After calling and qualifying Jeremiah, God got specific about what he would use Jeremiah to do: "Then the Lord stretched out His hand and touched my mouth, and the Lord said to me. Behold, I have put My words in you mouth. See, I have appointed you this day over nations and over the kingdoms, To pluck up and to break down, To destroy and to overthrow, To build and to plant" (Jeremiah 1:9–10). God was calling Jeremiah to serve as a prophet and a charismatic leader calling for change. God then dealt with Jeremiah's vision: "And the word of the LORD came to me saying, What do you see, Jeremiah? And I said, I see a rod of an almond tree. Then the LORD said to me, You have seen well, for I am watching over My word to perform it" (Jeremiah 1:11–12).

God aligned Jeremiah's vision with his so Jeremiah might more clearly understand not only his calling but also God's mission. In the same way, I believe God desires that we see his vision for his church more clearly. We need a clear vision of how God wants to fulfill his mission of kingdom advancement through the church. A church that tears down ungodly divisions in the world aligns with God's vision for the church. The church of the New Testament deals with the dividing wall of Jew and Gentile, and today's church must deal with the dividing wall of race. The people of God in Jeremiah's day were not aligned with God because they had gone another way. Their hearts were someplace else, and they were worshipping other gods.

The issue today is that we have lost sight of the fact that the first Christian churches in scripture were multi-ethnic and missional. Race has blurred our vision so that when we read scripture, we read it with Black and White eyes. And because the White eyes are culturally dominant, we see a White church in scripture instead of a multi-ethnic church. Jeremiah saw things in his day as they really were, and he was able to see things as God desired them to be. We need the same kind of vision today. We need to see the church today as it is. For the most part, the church today is a segregated institution in an increasingly multi-ethnic world. Even in some churches with some diversity, the dominant group forces the other groups to assimilate into their culture even if that dominant group (particularly Whites) isn't fully aware that this is happening. There are also second- and third-generation ethnic churches that are actually functioning as White churches regardless of their ethnicity.

How to Move the Church Forward

To move forward toward where the church should be, we need to be willing to see it as it is and the ways it is failing to hear the multi-ethnic and missional. I do so by looking at the three Cs that describe it: crisis, captivity, and comfortable.

Crisis

In 2008, David T. Olson, at the time the national church planting director for the Evangelical Covenant church, published his book, The American Church in Crisis, in which he provided the first C for us: crisis. He wrote:

> The American church is in crisis. At first glance this may not be apparent, but while many signs of its evident success and growth abound, in reality the American church is losing

ground as the population continues to surge. . . . In reality the church in America is not booming, it is in crisis. On any given Sunday, the vast majority of Americans are absent from church. Even more troublesome, as the American population continues to grow, the church falls further and further behind"[1]

Olson uses research conducted by the American Church Research Project in 2005 to show the extent of the crisis. In that year, less than 17.5 percent of the American population was attending church on any given weekend: 9.1 percent attended the evangelical church, 3.0 percent the mainline church, and 5.3 percent the Catholic church. One of the key issues connected to this crisis of the church is that church growth continues to lag far behind population growth in the United States.

After focusing on the crisis of the American church, Olson turned to the opportunities for the church and provided a solution to the crisis by calling the church to healthy growth through the "natural result of the gospel working in peoples' lives. Churches should bear fruit, both by inward change in the lives of believers and in outward change through conversion, community transformation, and global impact."[2] He was, in effect, calling for the church to be missional in order to address the crisis that it was in because the church is healthy when there is conversion and spiritual growth. According to Olson, the church is missional when it's about community transformation locally and making a global impact.

Olson then identified church planting as a central strategy for developing missional churches to reach the majority of Americans who are not in church on any given weekend. Through church planting, the crisis of the church can become a kingdom-advancing opportunity. For Olson, the issue wasn't just about population growth in and of itself but how it is growing:

> As the first of the baby boomer generation approaches retirement, the emerging generation and the growing non-Anglo populations require new and creative church-planting models. Multi-ethnicity is the most important and challenging growth edge in church planting. Over the last 15 years, many denominations have been actively engaged in planting new churches in a variety of ethnic communities. Because the future will bring increased diversity in America, planting more first and second-generation ethnic congregations will be crucial. Planting intentional multi-ethnic congregations (made up of two or more ethnicities) will also be important for both theological and practical reasons.[3]

Olson ended the book by making the case for the multi-ethnic and missional church as the solution to the church in crisis. I wholeheartedly agree with him. But if we continue to plant and revitalize churches in the same old way, we risk diving further into crisis. We cannot look at the crisis of the church and simply apply recycled models of the Black and White church. Instead, the post-Black, post-White church offers a new approach for engaging the social realities around us for kingdom advancement.

The church's ability to advance the kingdom of God will be limited if the majority of churches continue to be racially and ethnically segregated. This is the practical reason for the multi-ethnic church. As we look at the growing and diverse population around us, why wouldn't we aggressively pursue those who are lost and hurting no matter what their ethnicity?

The work being done by the Pacific Southwest Conference of the Evangelical Covenant church, of which I am superintendent, serves as an illustration. The Pacific Southwest Conference, which covers California, Arizona, Hawaii, Nevada, and Utah, was formed as a mission region of the Evangelical Covenant church in 1902. Like the denomination, the conference was originally formed as mission society of sorts. The five original churches were located in California and made up of Swedish immigrant families. We currently have 164 Covenant churches within this area, and over half of them are less than twenty-five years old. This growth came about because of a strong focus on church planting in the 1990s under Olson's leadership. Currently our churches have a combined weekend worship attendance of about forty-five thousand people, and about 70 percent of them are European-American. So from a racial standpoint, we are a predominantly White region. Yet some important information about this region of the United States is relevant here. First, it is in the midst of an urban explosion: twelve of the top fifty largest cities in America are in our region; among them are Los Angeles, Phoenix, San Francisco, Las Vegas, Tucson, and Sacramento.[4] We also have five of the top twenty-five metropolitan areas in the nation: Los Angeles–Long Beach–Riverside, San Jose–San Francisco–Oakland, San Diego–Carlsbad–San Marcos, all in California; and Phoenix–Mesa–Scottsdale in Arizona.[5]

Arizona and California are examples of the population growth in our future. Arizona's population is 6.3 million today, but by 2050 it will be somewhere between 10 and 14 million. California has a population close to 38 million. By 2050 the population will be around 60 million.

Now let's look at population growth within our region in the context of ethnicity. In California, 43.2 percent of Californians speak a language other than English at home: 89 percent of California immigrants are from Latin America or Asia. Hispanics make up 35.5 percent of the state's total population, and by 2050 they will be 52 percent. Asian-Americans currently are 12.4 percent of the state's population; they will grow to 13 percent by 2050. Here's where it gets interesting for the Black and White church in California: African-Americans, now 6.1 percent, will drop to 5 percent by 2050. And European-Americans, currently at 43 percent, will drop to 26 percent by 2050.

This information shows us that addressing the crisis of the church into the future is not just about church planting. Our conference's focus on church planting in the last twenty-five years has brought some diversity to the conference: in our overall weekend attendance, we are 30 percent non-White. We are clearly a multi-ethnic denominational region. But we can do more. We will have to be intentional about planting multi-ethnic and missional churches, especially in larger metropolitan areas. We also have to develop revitalization efforts that help us work with existing churches to become multi-ethnic. We have to develop the capacity of these churches to transform lives and communities in the growing multicultural reality surrounding them. The future of California alone makes a strong case for the post-Black, post-White church, but it's true for the rest of the country too.

According to U.S. Census Bureau projections, by midcentury, the nation will be more racially and ethnically diverse. Minorities, now roughly one-third of the U.S. population, are expected to become the majority in 2042, with the nation projected to be 54 percent minority in 2050. By 2050, the minority population, which means everyone except for non-Hispanic, single-race Whites, is projected to be 235.7 million out of a total of 439 million. Whites are projected to lose population in the 2030s and 2040s and comprise 46 percent of the total population in 2050, down from 66 percent in 2008. Meanwhile, the Hispanic population is projected to nearly triple, from 46.7 million to 132.8 million between 2008 and 2050. Its share of the nation's total population is projected to double, from 15 percent to 30 percent. The Black population is projected to increase from 41.1 million, or 14 percent of the population in 2008, to 65.7 million or 15 percent in 2050. The Asian population is projected to climb from 15.5 million to 40.6 million, from 5.1 percent to 9.2 percent.[6]

Recent population growth by race and ethnicity shows that these projections are already becoming reality. In the United States, all major racial groups increased in population size between 2000 and 2010, but they grew at different rates. Over the decade, the Asian population experienced the fastest rate of growth, and the White population experienced the slowest rate. The total U.S. population grew by 9.7 percent, from 281.4 million in 2000 to 308.7 million in 2010. More than half of the growth in the total population was due to the increase in the Hispanic community. In 2010, there were 50.5 million Hispanics in the United States, composing 16 percent of the total population, up from 35.3 million (or 13 percent) in 2000. The Hispanic population's increase between 2000 and 2010 accounts for over half of the 27.3 million increase in the total population of the United States.[7] Seventy-five percent of the Hispanic population in the United States resides in eight states: Arizona, California, Colorado, Florida, Illinois, New Jersey, New York, and Texas.[8] The White population increased at a slower rate than the total population in recent years. The White population grew by only 6 percent, from 211.5 million to 223.6 million. But while the White population increased numerically over the ten-year period, its total population declined from 75 percent to 72 percent of the total.[9] The Black population increased by 12 percent, from 34.7 million to 38.9 million, a faster rate than the total population.[10]

This is the reality that surrounds the church in the United States. Our urban, multi-ethnic, and multiracial culture is also in crisis: economic, social, and cultural. The family is in trouble, and school systems are struggling. Through music and social media, we continue to see images glorifying violence, greed, the pursuit of power at any cost, and a search for identity primarily in sexuality. The church must be the solution to the crisis around it. In the Gospel of Matthew, we read about the way Jesus dealt with a crisis situation:

> And when they came to the multitude, a man came up to Him, falling on his knees before Him, and saying, Lord, have mercy on my son, for he is a lunatic, and is very ill; for he often falls into the fire, and often into the water. And I brought him to Your disciples, and they could not cure him. And Jesus answered and said, O unbelieving and perverted generation, how long shall I be with you? How long shall I put up with you? Bring him to Me. And Jesus rebuked him, and the demon came out of him, and the boy was cured at once. Then the disciples came to Jesus privately and said, Why could we not cast it out? And He said to them, Because of the littleness of your faith; for truly I say to you, if you have the faith as a mustard seed, you shall say to this mountain, Move from here to there and it shall move; and nothing shall be impossible to you. But this kind does not go out except by prayer and fasting [Matthew 17:14–20].

In this situation of a boy with an evil spirit, the father brought the boy to the followers of Jesus, but they weren't able to address this challenge. The father then brought the boy directly to Jesus, and Jesus cured him. This alone makes the story powerful. But this is not what God was trying to show us. The main focus of this story is that the followers of Jesus were not able to address the boy's crisis. Jesus expected his followers to be able to deal with the issues that arise from the multitude of people around them. In fact he empowered them. This was part of kingdom-advancing work.

Today God looks at the diversity within the communities surrounding the churches of America. He sees the challenges and the crisis facing this great multi-ethnic and multicultural multitude. He sees at-risk youth, unemployment, racial division. He sees it all, and with a heart of compassion. Because he looks to the church to deal with all the issues of the multitude, through the Holy Spirit, he desires to equip and empower the church to engage the issues of the multitude in order that lives and communities might be transformed.

The church should not be daunted by the diversity and the challenges in the world around us. God empowers us to advance the kingdom no matter where we are: city, suburb, or small town. We must allow God to give us a passion for changing the communities around us and empower us to extend his love, grace, and truth to the multi-ethnic multitudes. We can't address this crisis if we are in crisis ourselves.

The first C is thus crisis: the church is not keeping up with the diversity of the growing population. The second C that hinders us from advancing the kingdom is captivity.

Captivity *to the culture around us*

Former multi-ethnic church pastor and current professor of evangelism Soong-Chan Rah states that the church is in captivity, which he defines in this way:

> The phrase *captivity of the church* points to the danger of the church being defined by an influence other than the Scriptures. The church remains the church, but we more accurately reflect the culture around us than the characteristics of the bride of Christ. We are held captive to the culture that surrounds us. To speak of the white captivity of the church is an acknowledgement that white culture has dominated, shaped, and captured Christianity in the United States. At times, the white evangelical church has been enmeshed with Western, white American culture to the great detriment of the spread of the gospel.[11]

Rah shows us that the church cannot engage the culture to advance if it's enslaved to the values of the dominant culture. Some of the dominant values in the United States are individualism, consumerism, and materialism. In order for the church to engage the culture for transformation, it needs to embrace biblical values such as community, generosity, and bearing the burdens of others. The church can easily find itself in an internal battle between the values it desires to live out and the ones it actually does by being held culturally captive.

Subcultural values also influence the broader culture. Hip-hop culture is one of these subcultures that I have written about in the past. This culture was created by mostly African-American youth in the Bronx in the 1970s and was intended to serve as an artistic alternative to youth violence and other negative activities. The original principles that shaped its value system were peace, love, community, and having fun. By the late 1980s, hip-hop culture had moved beyond an urban and Black art form to become the universal music, language, and fashion of an entire generation.

Subcultures can be powerfully influential movements, but they don't compare in power to the dominant Western and White cultural influences. Not all of these dominant cultural values are bad, of course, but they become a problem when they capture the church and become more influential than scripture. Because Western and White cultural influences are dominant in the broader society and the White church is a dominant influence in the church world, it is important to know how they connect to one another. Rah helps us to see these points.

First, Rah says, the church is being held captive by the Western philosophy of individualism: "The American church, in taking its cues from Western, white culture, has placed at the center of its theology and ecclesiology the primacy of the individual. The cultural captivity of the church has meant that the church is more

Vs community

likely to reflect the individualism of Western philosophy than the value of community found in Scripture."[12]

Taking personal responsibility for one's life is not a bad thing, and seeing ourselves individually as God's beloved child isn't either. We come to Christ repenting of our individual sins and in turn receive grace, forgiveness, and new life. But if we focus too much on the individual, we overlook the emphasis on community that is clear throughout scripture. The church at the end of the day is a community, not an institution full of individuals. If the White church especially is going to become a post-White church, it must understand more deeply the high value that other cultures place on community. Having a stronger focus on community is both biblical and relevant to reaching a diverse society.

Most of the ideas we get from scripture to support individualism are mainly limited to small portions of scripture in the New Testament. We can look at what is known as the "fruits of the spirit," which call us individually to be loving, joyful, patient, and kind (Galatians 5:22). But much more is written about the primacy of community within the scriptures. The Bible begins when God creates humanity. He recognizes that man should not live alone, so he creates woman, and they are placed in the Garden of Eden, a community. In the book of Exodus, a community, the nation of Hebrews cries out to God for their deliverance from oppression in Egypt. God delivers this community and makes a covenant with them in the wilderness. He then leads this community toward the promised land. In the book of Acts in the New Testament, we see the first church develop as a community:

> And they were continually devoting themselves to the apostles'
> teaching and to fellowship, to the breaking of bread, and to
> prayer. And everyone kept feeling a sense of awe; and many
> wonders and signs were taking place through the apostles.
> And all those who had believed were together, and had all

things in common; and they began selling their property and possessions, and were sharing them with all, as anyone might have need. And day by day continuing with one mind in the temple, and breaking bread from house to house, they were taking their meals together with gladness and sincerity of heart, praising God and having favor with all the people. And the Lord was adding to their number day by day those who were being saved [Acts 2:42–47].

In much of the White church, preaching, teaching, and ministry initiatives focus on the individual: being a good spouse, parent, child, or single person living faithfully. The focus can also be on individualized topics such as being a person of integrity and character. And topics are focused on the individual and God centered around prayer and Bible study. But too much of this focus can lead to the development of ministry initiatives that meet the needs of individual families or single individuals instead of missional ministries focused on equipping a faith community to become vehicles of transformation in the world.

I've read books on church planting and church growth where a picture of an upper-middle-class White male is used to represent the target audience of the church. Basically the strategy is to reach individuals and meet their needs, and the church will grow as a result. Because the target individual is upper middle class, the focus is on developing ministry programs that reach the spiritual need of this person. Because he has plenty of material resources, there's no need to worry about economic or financial well-being.

In order to reach the family as well, the church then focuses on the individual needs of the spouse through a women's ministry and then a children's and youth ministry. I an not against the church having strong ministry initiatives focused on women, children, and youth. The question is, What values are driving these ministry initiatives?

In a culture so influenced by individualism, the church must hone in on the development of healthy and Christ-centered community. Most churches today recognize this and have responded to this need through initiatives like Alpha, which takes a more communal approach to evangelism, small groups, and Christian formation. These kinds of initiatives present the Christian as one created by God with gifts and abilities intended to bring about change and transformation. Our Christian lives are not our own; they are to be lived out for the sake of others in need of the liberation that comes from a relationship with a loving God and loving people.

The challenge for the church is building community cross-culturally in these areas. How do we serve as evangelists in an increasingly multicultural world? The church must equip and empower people for this task. We have to be willing to explore how individualism keeps the church from being multi-ethnic and missional. For example, individualism keeps the church from acknowledging the broader corporate and systemic issues that divide ethnic and racial groups. We tend to see issues of race and ethnicity from an individual perspective. As Rah says, "The excessive individualism of the Western, white cultural captivity of the church reduces racism to an exclusively personal issue. Evangelicalism's capacity to excessive individualism means outrage for the corporate sin of racism is rarely present."[13]

The second chapter of Acts shows the power and outcomes of a stronger communal orientation within the church. Learning, praying, and eating with others allow us to see God's working in other people. We also get the opportunity, if we're focused on more than ourselves, to see the needs of others and be presented with the glorious opportunity to respond through sacrificial giving, an act of worship in the church.

We live in a world where we are forced to think of ourselves all the time. We have to think about our individual performance at work, taking care of our homes, and our individual families. I have to pay my individual bills. When I'm driving on the highway, I have to look out for my own safety. Shouldn't church be at least one place where I can be freed from the obsession of thinking of just myself or just my family? A radical, communal approach to church gives me the blessed opportunity to see the needs, stories, victories, and struggles of others. Seeing others cross-culturally works to dismantle and then destroy my prejudices. But excessive individualism can lead me to blame others for their failings or problems instead of having the compassion that Jesus had when he saw the issues of the diverse multitudes. Jesus could have looked at the people and blamed each individually for being lost, sick, paralyzed, or demon possessed. But he didn't. It's easy for me as a middle-class, highly educated person to look at those around me who are struggling and of a different ethnicity and think, *Why didn't they go to college, get a job, and work hard like I did?* The compassion of Jesus living in me through the Holy Spirit changes my heart and thinking as I live in the multi-ethnic community of the post-Black, post-White church. Developing deep relationships in church across ethnicity and race boundaries changes how I interact with people of different ethnicities and races in all aspects of my life.

We also see in the first church in Acts a connection between strong community and significant evangelistic growth. As the community ate together, worshipped together, and met one another's needs, God added to their number. The development of a strong Christ-centered and multi-ethnic community leads to greater evangelistic impact in our increasingly multicultural reality.

Rah then goes on to discuss how consumerism and materialism hold the church captive:

Materialism and consumerism govern the way we live our lives and how we relate to each other in society. Materialism and consumerism reduce people to a commodity. An individual's worth in society is based upon what assets they bring and what possessions they own. . . . Materialism also creates a sense of urgency in having our personal needs met. Because everything has a price and can be made affordable, we have been conditioned to expect quick and easy answers to problems. These answers always come in the material realm and we begin to believe that our spiritual problems can be solved with material goods. . . . The Western, white captivity of the church means that the church has wholeheartedly adapted the materialistic and consumeristic worldview of American culture. To be a good American Christian means to be both a good capitalist and a good consumer within that capitalist system.[14]

We can't separate materialism and consumerism from individualism. Television floods us with commercials telling us that we're inadequate on some level individually and need to purchase something to remedy those deficits. The commercials tell us that we're individually overweight, not educated enough, don't have enough hair, don't drive the right car, and, if you're single, haven't met the right person yet. Buying something material seems to be the solution for whatever problem we have.

When the financial crisis of our country was just beginning, when George W. Bush was president, the initial solution was to stimulate the economy by giving American citizens tax breaks, which, the president hoped, would lead them to spend money. That's the core of our American culture, spend money on products, and it leads to a culture of commodification. When the church is held captive by materialism and consumerism, it ends up living under the pressure to produce ministry initiatives such as worship, children's ministry, and youth ministry as programmatic products in order to draw in consumers. Add to this the fact that the most visible expression of the church is Black or White, and without even realizing it, the church is in the business of selling ministry products to a mostly Black or White audience. Other ethnic groups have to buy into these ministry products even if they don't deal with what they're going through because there's no other choice.

Christian music is a good example. For the most part, Christian music today is broken down into Black and White, even if we don't use the term Black or White to describe these categories. We use terms such as *contemporary Christian music* with music centers in places like Nashville and Austin and *urban gospel* with centers in Detroit and Atlanta. There was a time when urban gospel was called Black gospel music, but we've become a little more politically correct (this may be something else holding the church captive). There have been some exceptions from time to time in Christian music, mostly through Hispanic groups such as the Katinas and Salvador. For the most part, though, Christian music can be broken down to Black or White. This is the music that is promoted to us and that we buy as Christians. It also influences the type of music we sing on Sunday morning in many churches. And many people use that music to decide whether to leave that church or remain part of it. I have talked with pastors who have been forced to fire the worship leader in their church because a small but vocal and well-resourced group of people complained about the music.

Worship has become a commodity, and so has preaching. When I served as a pastor in Minneapolis, people would make decisions to join or leave the church many times over a single sermon. I remember one couple who joined the church because they were so moved over the sermon I preached the first Sunday they visited. They came up to me after the worship service and said, "We're in!" Three months later, because of something I said in the sermon that wasn't even the main point, I received a phone call letting me know that they were moving on because of what I'd said.

Attendance and offerings become elements of transaction in a church held captive by materialism and consumerism. This is the connection between materialism, consumerism, and individualism: I will choose to show up at a church and give to it if it meets my individual tastes and needs. Many times this sense of our individual tastes and needs is connected to our racial identity. Without realizing it, our desire to get our individual tastes and needs met can cause our participation in systemic racism.

Rah offers the sin of racism as another aspect of Western culture that is holding the church captive. He deals with both the individual and corporate expressions and outcomes of racism in our society and presents White privilege as one of the main ways that racism holds the church captive:

> Acknowledging the corporate responsibility and culpability of the sin of racism can lead to the revelation of the system of white privilege, a system that oftentimes goes unrecognized in the dialogue on race. The explicit expression of the sin of race is still evident in American society, but it has also taken a more subtle form in the expression of white privilege. . . . White privilege is the system that places white culture in American society at the center with all other cultures on the fringes. . . . While North America is becoming more and more multiethnic and we are seeing more nonwhite cultural expressions, white culture remains as the primary standard by which all other cultures are judged. An unfair advantage and privilege, therefore, is given to whites in a society that reveres and prioritizes them.[15]

I deal with race and racism in more detail in Chapter Four, but it is important to mention here that we cannot deal with the issue of race and the church without addressing White privilege. Unfortunately, this is the toughest part of dealing with race because it tends to put European-Americans on the defensive. White privilege is interpreted as saying that all Whites are racists, and who wants to admit that? I don't believe that all White people are racists, but White privilege is a separate matter. Rah is really pointing to the benefit of being White in a racialized society. The ideologies, philosophies, and theologies of Whiteness help put the White church at the center of all discussions. If you were to ask people to identify the pastors and theologians who are influencing the church in general, you will get in response White names, such as Rob Bell, John Piper, and N. T. Wright. Since the White church is presented as the right church, books and conferences on church development focus mainly on White church models. This is how you get second- and third-generation ethnic churches functioning as White churches instead of forging creative and culturally unique models of church that can better reach into the multicultural reality.

I'm not saying that it is minority churches alone that need to be freed from White captivity, and neither is Rah. Rah is really pleading for the liberation of the so-called White church, specifically, the evangelical White church. Whiteness is not good for the so-called White church. This is why I'm presenting the post-White church as a way to freedom. This freedom for the White church begins with looking back to its immigrant and ethnic past in order to live into a new multi-ethnic future. In fact, groups known today as Whites at one time were referred to using their ethnic designations: Irish, German, Russian, Swedish, and so forth. And in many cases in the past, divisions and prejudice existed between these groups.

Ethnic group is actually a more biblically rooted identity than White. In scripture, you don't see the racial term *White* used to describe people, but there are times when European ethnicities are used, such as a person being Roman or Greek. Becoming post-White begins with recognizing Whiteness as unbiblical. The rich heritage in the immigrant and ethnic pasts of so-called Whites can serve as a source for developing a multi-ethnic and missional church. I give this more attention in Chapter Four on race. But first we move on to the final C: comfortable.

Comfort

A great concern that I have for the church is that it is comfortable: people seem satisfied with the declining and segregated church. At least, it seems so from their actions. The mainline denominations have been in decline for a decade. Some of its leaders appear to have accepted the decline and don't seem to have a collective sense of urgency about it.

I must admit that I have met with pastors and church leaders in evangelical and mainline churches who don't like the condition their church is in right now. But when I start talking about what it will take to turn the church around, specifically becoming missional within an increasingly diverse surrounding community, they push back. Even if a struggling church is dissatisfied, the thought of radical change for kingdom advancement seems too much bear. In some cases, a church may develop a false sense of comfort in order to push past dissatisfaction. Sometimes this can be more about issues of power. In small churches especially, three families might be more comfortable with the power they have in keeping the church where it is versus growing by becoming multi-ethnic and missional.

Being large and well resourced can also make a church comfortable. Why would a large White church full of resources and a large staff feel it needs to change? You could ask the same question of a Black megachurch. A large homogeneous church in the United States has become a symbol of success. It's hard to feel uncomfortable when the Christian culture around you is telling you that you've made it. But just being large does not mean you are a healthy and missional church. Being large doesn't mean you are fulfilling the biblical mandate for making disciples. And purposely keeping your church small through the comfort found in having power is no more healthy or missional. Both models can produce false fruit. Being large develops the false fruit that kingdom advancement is gauged in numbers only. Staying small creates the false fruit that the kingdom of God is about meeting the needs of a small group of people by keeping them in power. Being satisfied with false fruit creates a comfort that sustains the church as we know it, and it is not conducive for kingdom advancement in today's realities.

As long as the church does not look like the place where we will live eternally, we should be uncomfortable. As long as only 20 percent or less of Americans are in a church on any given weekend, we should be uncomfortable. As long the primary picture of the church in America is a segregated one, we should feel uncomfortable. But we must do more than live in the state of being uncomfortable. We must let that feeling lead us to a more spirit-filled passion and urgency for the multi-ethnic multitude around us.

The Three Cs and the Future

The church today is characterized by crisis, captivity, and comfort. Moreover, the majority of the multi-ethnic multitudes in this nation are not in church. It's not because in the deeper core of their being many of them don't yearn for a personal relationship with God. It's not because there isn't a hunger for love, community, and a life of significance within our society. It's because in too many cases, the church isn't positioned well enough to reach them. Nevertheless, God still desires to use the church as the primary vehicle to advance his kingdom in the world and liberate us from our captivity. God can and will equip us by transforming our churches in multi-ethnic and missional communities. Our transformation will lead to the transformation of those in the communities around us.

3

compassion, mercy, and justice

A church that is truly missional is about ministries of compassion, mercy, and justice, both locally and globally. This work is a crucial part of kingdom advancement. The church tends to understand this globally, but it doesn't always live into this work within its surrounding community. As I have walked the streets of many inner-city communities around the country, I have seen homelessness, gang activity, boarded-up buildings, and drug users staggering down the sidewalks. At the same time, I notice church buildings almost wherever I look, and I wonder, "How can this community be in turmoil when there are so many churches in the area?" Being missional locally means taking a holistic approach to ministry that connects evangelism and outreach in a way that leads to kingdom justice. That justice occurs when a person or a group has not only responded to the gift of eternal life but is equipped and empowered for living a life of missional purpose right now. The missional church ought to lead to missional lives in the surrounding community. Ministries of compassion, mercy, and justice become the glue for connecting evangelism and outreach that lead to deeper transformation.

Compassion, mercy, and justice have been part of a more holistic approach to ministry in global missions for a while now. Consider the work of Compassion International, a global ministry dedicated to the long-term development of children living in poverty around the world. In 2010, I had the opportunity to travel to Nairobi, Kenya, on what is called a compassion trip, with some pastors of churches within the denominational region where I serve. During the week-long trip, we traveled to a number of sites to see how Compassion's child sponsorship programs, in partnership with local churches, were dealing with the crisis of extreme poverty.

This wasn't my first trip with the group. Two years earlier, I had been on a similar trip to El Salvador, and I have also been a speaker on behalf of the organization for a number of years, going to Christian college campuses, music festivals, youth conferences, and pastors' conferences and challenging people to make the monthly financial sacrifice to address poverty through child sponsorship. The sponsorship is the vehicle to a holistic child development initiative that addresses poverty by dismantling it generationally. A sponsor who provides education, health care, and skills for children to have fruitful lives can potentially end poverty within their family and even in a whole community if those children take on a leadership role. There is also a focus on spiritual development through the organization's partnering with local churches. This holistic approach cares for the spirit, souls, and bodies of a child and his or her family.

A Holistic Approach to Ministry

Two questions are at the core of a practical theology for a holistic approach to ministry: If you equip someone through education and skills but that person doesn't know Jesus as his or her Lord and Savior, what difference does that make? And if you share Christ with someone and that person accepts him as Lord and Savior but lacks the skills and access to a life of empowerment and purpose, what difference does that really make? Both questions must be fully answered if a ministry is to be holistic.

My passion for this approach to ministry led me to Compassion International early in this new century. I had been involved in a holistic and missional approach to ministry in local communities where I'd lived for awhile, but I wanted to be apart of something global.

The trip to Kenya was not my first trip to Africa. In summer 2001, I had gone to South Africa with my wife, Donecia, to speak at a youth development conference put on by Youth for Christ. We got off the plane and made our way to baggage claim where a small group of people met us. One of their leaders looked at us and with outstretched arms said, "Welcome home." It was such a powerful moment that my wife and I began to cry. As this leader hugged us both, he said, "This is the motherland, and this is your home." As a descendent of African slaves, I know that South Africa is probably not where my ancestors came from, but Africa remains the continent of my heritage. On my mother's side, I can trace my heritage back to a slave girl named Ginny. I have been told that she was also called Easter by some. So although she was a slave, she was referred to as Resurrection Sunday. For me, this is powerful because it gives me further ethnic identity as one from a people that rose from the grave of slavery.

By the time I returned to Africa to visit Kenya, I had high expectations. On my first trip to Africa, I didn't know what to expect. This time I went with an expectation to learn about the great diversity, beauty, spirituality, and challenges on what some call the Motherland. And this second trip met those expectations and more. The Kenya experience strengthened my ethnic identity. We traveled around and outside Nairobi visiting Compassion International's ministry sites. Each site was located in an area of extreme, and heartbreaking, poverty. Each place also provided a picture of great hope through the holistic ministries of local churches. We never saw Compassion's name at any of the sites because the local churches were at the center of the work. These churches not only met for worship services but were also running tutoring programs and job training initiatives, and they were equipping families with skills to build a healthy community.

One of the sites we went to was in Dandora, a suburb. In the United States, suburbs are normally the most prosperous places within a larger metropolitan area, and our poverty tends to be concentrated in inner cities and rural areas. We saw the opposite in Kenya. Dandora has the second largest concentration of poverty in Kenya. As we drove into Dandora, we saw a large trash dump. It's as if the town is built on mounds of garbage. I can't describe in words what I felt when I saw mothers, children, and pigs digging through the trash dump for food and other necessities. But we also found hope in Dandora at a local church that rescues babies and children from the trash dump.

A charismatic woman named Helen met us and led us into the sanctuary for a worship service. After some singing, the pastor of the church spoke to us, and then Helen shared the work they were doing with children, families, and women infected with HIV. Through its partnership with Compassion International, the church provided education, economic development initiatives, and health services. We heard testimony from a young man who had been rescued from the trash dump as a young child by the church and was now going to college. He had given his life to Christ and wanted to work with other churches in the area of community development after graduating. This church was truly missional, and it didn't separate evangelism from ministries of compassion, mercy, and justice.

The next day we visited another site, this one in a more remote rural area of Kenya. At the church we visited, led by the Masai, we again saw a holistic approach to ministry. We also saw young men perform a traditional dance that is a rite of passage for officially moving into manhood. As the boys danced in front of us, I again began to cry.

After the church leaders served us lunch, they called me and another African-American pastor within our group up front. The pastor and the head elder of the church made us honorary elders of the church and presented us with gifts. I was incredibly moved. I felt that I should be providing them with something, but they were giving gifts to me. I thought that I would be bringing a blessing, and yet I was being blessed beyond what I could have imagined before arriving. I felt the Holy Spirit in a powerful way during that moment as I was being ministered to. Once again, I couldn't hold back the tears.

Not until later that evening did I feel that I could explain to some of the others on the trip why I was crying. I started with the story of how my wife and I had been greeted in South Africa years earlier and how I connected that to being made an honorary elder in the Masai church. When I saw the boys dancing, I also thought of the boys I had seen the day before in Dandora. But there was more going in my heart that drove the tears down my face. I also thought of children I knew and had known back in the United States. I thought of young people involved in gangs in the community where I went to high school. I thought of children I met through a tutoring program I have participated in at an Oakland public elementary school since I moved to Northern California. I thought of youth who looked just like those Masai boys I had met in a juvenile detention center in Saint Paul, Minnesota. I couldn't separate the poverty and at-risk issues of youth in Africa from those of youth in the United States, and my heart was filled with concern and compassion for both. I was connected to the village of the Masai and my own villages back home.

The extreme poverty in places like Dandora and among some of the Masai people is much worse than, say, the west side of Chicago. Nevertheless, we must recognize the issues in our own back yards. Some of those I have shared this thought with have not known how to respond. Was I saying that the poverty we were witnessing in Kenya wasn't as important to me as the issues in Minneapolis or Oakland? Absolutely not. I was saying that I couldn't separate the issues in Kenya from similar ones in U.S. cities and rural areas.

As an evangelical, I often wonder how we can have such a heart for places like Kenya, the Congo, and Central America but not be willing to let the injustices in the United States break our hearts at the same level. It shouldn't be an either-or issue but a both-and. We can't let global poverty and injustice keep us from addressing local challenges and injustices. We need to stop having a different mind-set about global injustice and poverty than we have of local injustice and poverty. We may be far enough away from Africa that we don't feel responsible for the cause of poverty and injustice there, so we can move more quickly to the better feeling that comes from being part of the solution. We Americans like that: when we do a good deed, we feel good. When we can be the solution to a problem that we feel we didn't cause, we are the good guy in the story. We become superhero and savior.

This is one of the reasons evangelicals have been so good at global missions. We are good at going into a situation where there are lost and hurting people, and through the blessedness of having resources, we are able to do good works. But shouldn't we also want to do similarly good works here at home? We are more responsible and involved in the causes of poverty and injustice here, and we need to deal with that, just as we need to be less comfortable as a church.

I'm not against global missions. I believe that the church should be aggressively and prayerfully involved in global missions. But I also believe that the church should be involved in local missions within local communities as well. Being missional is about taking the missiology or the theology and practices we've applied to global missions and begin to apply them to our local approach to ministry.

A Mind-Set and a Mind Challenge

Another one of the reasons the church has had more traction at global missions is the economics of it. For less than forty dollars a month, my family can sponsor a child through Compassion International. From letters and pictures, we see the impact of our giving. Some of us get to go on a Compassion trip and see the impact of our monthly giving up close. So what seems to us in the United States as a relatively small amount of money can go a long way in a Third World country.

Dealing with disparities and poverty in this country is complex. Change can be slow and frustrating, and it can be expensive. Our financial sacrifice in this country may be limited to giving a couple of dollars to a homeless person holding a sign on the street or giving something to the Salvation Army as we leave a store during the holidays. But it also goes back to a mind-set and what I call a mind challenge. The mind-set is that many people believe that people in poverty or facing serious life challenges are there because of their own choices. We can also tend to believe that because our country provides opportunities for all Americans that people for the most part can turn their life around through the right individual choices. This gets back to Soong-Chan Rah's point of our being held captive to individualism. A mind-set of individualism makes it hard to accept that forces beyond individual choices can lead to poverty, crisis, and injustice.

It is also hard to accept that the way that we live our lives could be contributing in some way to what's going on around us. Could the choices that I make in terms of how I spend my money, how I run my business, how I participate in politics, and how I view people of a difference race or economic class contribute to sustaining communities and people who are underresourced?

Another part of the American culture contributing to this mind-set is the connection between prosperity and mobility. The more education we have, the more money we tend to make, which affords us the opportunity to move to communities where we can be around people like us. Prosperity provides the gift of access and mobility. Poverty cuts it off. When I was in Kenya, I saw this up close. I met many people who not only didn't have cars, they didn't have bicycles. Some didn't even have shoes and had never been outside their poverty-stricken community. But the same is true in some places in the United States. Some urban youth have never been outside their inner-city community. They've never been outside the gang activity, violence, boarded-up buildings, and overcrowded apartment complexes in their neighborhood. A trip for them may simply be catching the bus or subway to school. This doesn't compare to the deprivation I saw in Kenya, but it shouldn't be ignored either. No matter where we live, suburb or city, we must continue to find ways to be missional in local communities around us that face challenges.

We must allow God to change our mind-set and help us deal with the mind challenge concerning responsibility. Do we carry individually and collectively any responsibility for the disparities, crisis, and injustices within our own country? Are we responsible for the causes and the solutions? I believe the answer is yes. To make this point let's look at the book of Nehemiah in the Old Testament:

And they said to me, the remnant there in the province who survived the captivity are in great distress and reproach, and the wall of Jerusalem is broken down and its gates are burned with fire. Now it came about when I heard these words, I sat down and wept and mourned for days; and I was fasting and praying before the God of heaven. And I said, I beseech Thee, O LORD God of heaven, the great and awesome God, who preserves the covenant and loving-kindness for those who love Him and keep His commandments, let Thine ear now be attentive and Thine eyes open to hear the prayer of Thy servant which I am praying before Thee now, day and night on behalf of the sons and Israel Thy servants, confessing the sins of the sons of Israel which we have sinned against Thee; I and my father's house have sinned. We have acted very corruptly against Thee and have not kept the commandments, nor the statutes, nor the ordinances which Thou didst command Thy servant Moses.

And I said to the king (Artaxerxes), if it please the king, and if your servant has found favor before you, send me to Judah, to the city of my father's tomb, that I may rebuild it [Nehemiah 1:3–7, 2:4–5]

Nehemiah saw the crisis of the city in ruins and took responsibility for the position the city was in and for rebuilding it. He lived and worked outside the city, but he nevertheless took responsibility for its woes. He could have said, "I don't live down there. What's that got to do with me?" But he saw this city as his city and the people in it as his people.

Many people go to a church, but they don't feel any connection to the community surrounding that church because they live elsewhere (these churches are known as commuter churches). But this wasn't the case for Nehemiah. He had a heart for this city that was the closest place in crisis to him. This was his homeland. He prayed to God, repenting for the ways in which he was responsible, and also asked God to use him to get about the business of rebuilding the city.

What if members of a church had a greater missional heart for the lost and broken people in the surrounding community? What if that were just as important as (or even more important than) sustaining their church as it is? Nehemiah approached the king and asked for the resources to mobilize people to rebuild the city. This was both a marketplace and a political move on his part: he went to those with political power, resources, and skills to address the distant crisis. With permission from an earthly king, he went to the city in crisis to provide the solution: this was a missional move. He went to Jerusalem with a strategy to build beloved community. Being missional is seeing the crisis around us and taking responsibility through prayer and action. It is God who does the sending and we, as God's church, who are called to go.

If your church is in an affluent area, find the closest challenged area and become missional there, including partnering with a church in that area. With the recent economic crisis in the United States, you may not have to go far. A few years ago, the houses where I live, a suburb outside San Francisco, cost between $650,000 and $1 million. As the value of these houses has plummeted in the Great Recession, many have become rental properties and others are in foreclosure as I'm writing this chapter. What happens to the people when this financial devastation occurs in an upscale suburban community? I wonder how many people who own or owned these houses are currently unemployed, retired early, or are now working a job that caused them to take a pay cut? How has the financial strain affected their families? Sometimes financial strain and stress alone lead what looked like a healthy marriage toward divorce. If divorce is the case, how is this affecting the children? Are they now participating in risky behavior? Because of the increase in rental properties, this community may become attractive to some lower-income families who are able to pay their rent through a federal assistance program, and some middle-class families can now afford to buy houses in this community where they could not have in the past. Does this lead to greater multi-ethnic diversity?

It's easy to see how crisis can change a community fairly quickly. How can churches in such an area become more missional, more involved, and at the same time more multi-ethnic?

The story in the book of Nehemiah speaks to the church today. By engaging its surrounding community, the church can become more multi-ethnic and missional. Are we willing to take the same responsibility as Nehemiah did? We have a heavenly king who is willing to empower us to address the challenges of our communities. Taking responsibility for the solution may be less of a challenge for the mind than taking responsibility for why there are problems in the first place. This is one of the reasons that in America, it's easier to talk about the Holocaust than slavery or our historic treatment of Native Americans and Japanese-Americans. Why is it that we have a Holocaust museum in our nation's capital but not one dedicated to telling the story of slavery and Jim Crow segregation, so that in these parts of our history, we can say, "Never again"?

One of the tough things to deal with in the area of White privilege is the way in which Whites in general have benefited from the injustices of America's past. Moreover, some people believe that the only people who are engaged in racism and prejudice are those who are directly discriminating or oppressing another person or group of persons. The mind challenge here is to understand that it is possible not to be involved in a racist or discriminatory act yet still benefit from the systemic sin of racism. For example, some neighborhoods in the past excluded people of color from buying homes there. Surely some of the White families living in that type of neighborhood were not racist, yet they benefited from the discriminatory practice. The way that we can be transformed is by the renewing of our minds (Romans 12:2). Our view of the communities around us could have more to do with conforming to the cultural values of this world than with a transformed mind led by the Holy Spirit. A good first step in renewing the mind of the church around being missional is having a solid biblical foundation for compassion, mercy, and justice. The Holy Spirit can teach us and renew our minds through the word of God.

Biblical Foundations for Compassion, Mercy, and Justice

When Nehemiah was repenting to God through prayer, he mentioned Moses and the commandments, statutes, and ordinances that God gave him to share with the Israelites generations earlier. I begin to lay our biblical foundation with the book of Exodus in the Old Testament:

> And the angel of the LORD appeared to him in a blazing fire from the midst of a bush; and he looked, and behold, the bush was burning with fire, yet the bush was not consumed. So Moses said I must turn aside now and see this marvelous sight, why the bush is not burned up. When the LORD saw that he turned aside to look, God called to him from the midst of the bush, and said, Moses, Moses! And he said Here I am. Then He said, Do not come near here; remove your sandals from your feet, for the place on which you are standing is holy ground. He said also, I am the God of your father, the God of Abraham, the God of Isaac, and the god of Jacob. Then Moses hid his face, for he was afraid to look at God. And the LORD said, I have surely seen the affliction of My people who are in Egypt, and have given heed to their cry because of their taskmasters, for I am aware of their sufferings. So I have come down to

deliver them from the power of the Egyptians, and to bring them up from that land to a good and spacious land, to a land flowing with milk and honey, to the place of the Canaanite and the Hittite and the Amorite and the Perizzite and the Hivite and the Jebusite. And now, behold, the cry of the sons of Israel has come to Me; furthermore, I have seen the oppression with which the Egyptians are oppressing them. Therefore, come now, and I will send you to Pharaoh, so that you may bring My people, the sons of Israel, out of Egypt [Exodus 3:2–10].

In this text, we see a God who not only heard the cries of the oppressed but also responded by raising up a leader in Moses, who would lead them to freedom. Before leading the Israelites into freedom, though, God used Moses to confront Pharaoh and demand that he let the enslaved and oppressed Israelites go. We don't read in the beginning of Exodus that God authored and purposely designed the enslavement of the Israelites for some greater good. The Israelites were enslaved by a new pharaoh who had come into power. He didn't know the history of why they were living in Egypt and was intimidated by their population growth. Even the slavery of Joseph in the book of Genesis, which is the beginning of how the Israelites eventually ended up living among the Egyptians, happened initially because of the actions of Joseph's own brothers. God allowed his chosen people to be captured, exiled, and enslaved by various empires, but they occurred because of the Israelites' idolatry and freely chosen will not to live by the covenant that God made with them. But even in the midst of this, we see a loving God, a merciful God, and a God who delivers.

God sees oppression and hears the cries of the oppressed. He empowers leaders to confront those in power who develop and lead structures of oppression. He delivers the oppressed and desires relationship with them. This is biblical justice.

Recognizing justice in the scriptures ought to lead us to being comfortable with using the word justice in the church and doing the work of justice. We are called to be God's vehicles of justice in the world, as we see in Micah:

> With what shall I come to the LORD and bow myself before the God on high? Shall I come to Him with burnt offerings, with yearling calves? Does the LORD take delight in thousands of rams, in ten thousand rivers of oil? Shall I present my first-born for my rebellious acts, the fruit of my body for the sin of my soul? He has told you, O man what is good; and what does the LORD require of you but to do justice, to love kindness, and to walk humbly with your God [Micah 6:1–8]?

I bring this up because recently some social commentators have questioned whether social justice is biblical, and some have even boldly proclaimed that it is not. Conservative commentator Glenn Beck spent weeks in 2010 presenting social justice as unbiblical political socialism. He stated on both his television and radio shows at the time that anyone who is in church and hears the pastor use the term social justice needs to leave that church. He brought conservative and evangelical theologians on his television show to prove his belief that social justice is unbiblical.

I found this whole notion and effort quite sad because social justice clearly is biblical. If God sent Moses to go a political leader and publicly request justice for an oppressed people, is this not social justice? When the Israelites crossed the Red Sea and became free people, did this not alter the social fabric of their reality, as well as that of the Egyptians? Isn't the quest for justice what changes the social fabric? Social justice is biblical, and throughout the scriptures, we see it brought about by God. The story of Exodus inspired people in the United States to not only preach against slavery but to risk their lives fighting in a civil war to change the laws so that slavery would be abolished. The story also inspired the civil rights movement, and some have compared Martin Luther King Jr. to Moses.

God brought about justice for the Israelites and later in the wilderness made a covenant with them: "Now then, if you indeed obey My voice and keep My covenant, then you shall be My own possession among all the peoples, for all the earth is Mine; and you shall be a kingdom of priests and a holy nation" (Exodus 19:5–6).

In the wilderness God gave the Israelites a new identity. They were no longer slaves in Egypt but God's possession, a kingdom and a nation unto themselves. When God made the covenant with them in the wilderness through Moses, he presented to them the Ten Commandments. Half of the commandments are about how they were to relate to God and the other half about how they were to relate to one another. There were times when new generations of Israelites didn't live as a liberated and holy nation and lost sense of their heritage. And when this happened, God reminded them again:

> And now, Israel, what does the LORD your God require from you, but to fear the LORD your God, to walk in His ways and to love Him and to serve the LORD your God with all your heart and with all your soul, and to keep the LORD's commandments and His statutes which I am commanding you today for your good? Behold to the LORD your God belong the heaven and the highest heavens, the earth and all that is in it. Yet on your fathers did the LORD set His affection to love them, and He chose their descendants after them, even you above all peoples, as it is this day. Circumcise then your heart, and stiffen your neck no more. For the LORD your God is the God of gods and the LORD of lords, the great, the mighty, and the awesome God who does not show partiality, nor take a bribe. He executes justice for the orphan and the widow, and shows His love for the alien by giving him food and clothing. Show your love for the alien, for you were aliens in the land of Egypt [Deuteronomy 10:12–19].

God reminded the people that he was a God of justice, and executing justice was part of his mission in the world. He let the Israelites know that they were to participate in his mission in the world as God's chosen people because they were a missional people. God also calls them to become a chosen and missional people of justice. Throughout the books of Moses (that is, the first five books in the Bible), we see God reminding the Israelites that he delivered them out of oppression, that he made a covenant with them, and that they were to be a people of justice. He connected their being a people of justice with celebrations to remind them of their deliverance from slavery:

> Observe the month of Abib and celebrate the Passover to the LORD your God, for in the month of Abib the LORD your God brought you out of Egypt by night . . .

> Then you shall celebrate the Feast of Weeks to the LORD your God with a tribute of a freewill offering of your hand, which you shall give just as the LORD your God blesses you; and you shall rejoice before the LORD your God, you and your son and your daughter and your male and female servants and the Levite who is in your town, and the stranger and the orphan, and the widow who are in your midst, in the place where the LORD your God chooses to establish His name. And you shall remember that you were a slave in Egypt, and you shall be careful to observe these statutes [Deuteronomy 16:1, 110–12].

Being a people of justice in their context was about caring for the poor, the orphans, the widows, and the foreigners among them. I put emphasis on "among them." This was not a global missions venture. This was about doing justice among their own vulnerable, marginalized, and outcast. God also spoke to them through Moses about the ways of doing justice with those among them. That might mean sacrificing resources or forgiving debts owed. This justice for the most vulnerable was part of the laws or commands God gave to the people and about how they were to be in covenant with one another. So to this degree, being missional locally was an extension of the covenant they had with God and one another:

> You shall not oppress a hired servant who is poor and needy, whether he is one of your countrymen or one of your aliens who is in your land in your towns . . .

> You shall not pervert the justice due an alien or an orphan, nor take a widow's garment in pledge. But you shall remember that you were a slave in Egypt, and that the LORD your God redeemed you from there; therefore I am commanding you to do this thing. When you reap your harvest in your field and have forgotten a sheaf in the field, you shall not go back to get it; it shall be for the alien, for the orphan, and for the widow, in order that the LORD your God may bless you in all the work of your hands. When you beat your olive tree, you shall not go over the boughs again; it shall be for the alien, for the orphan, and for the widow. When you gather the grapes of your vineyard, you shall not go over it again; it shall be for the alien, for the orphan, and for the widow. And you shall remember that you were a slave in the land of Egypt; therefore I am commanding you to do this thing [Deuteronomy 24:14, 17–22].

When Jesus came to the earth as the Son of God, he proclaimed and provided a picture of the kingdom of God, and justice was included in this proclamation. Jesus as the fulfiller of the law did not abandon the call to justice: "The Spirit of the LORD is upon Me because He anointed me to preach the gospel to the poor. He has sent Me to proclaim release to the captives, and recovery of sight to the blind, to set free those who are downtrodden, to proclaim the favorable year of the LORD" (Luke 4:18–19).

I do not want to downplay in any way the importance of Jesus coming to bring new life through salvation. Jesus comes as the Son of God, as the Lamb that is to be slain on the cross for our sins. Through his shed blood, we have access to a new covenant and eternal life. Our eternity is ultimately the greatest gift from the Father through the Son. We have been delivered from a form of slavery as well. We have been set free from the slavery of sin and the sting of death. But we must also remember that God desires to use us to reach others who are still the walking dead in their sins—those who have yet to experience new life and gain an understanding of eternal life. This is the root of our passion for evangelism. We must also remember the call to compassion, mercy, and justice. Jesus connected justice to his kingdom proclamation so that biblical justice becomes kingdom justice. If there is still any doubt about Jesus connecting the kingdom of god to compassion, mercy, and justice, consider the conclusion of Matthew 25:

> But when the Son of Man comes in glory, and all the angels with Him, then He will sit on His glorious throne. And all the nations will be gathered before Him; and He will separate them from one another, as the shepherd separates the sheep from the goats; and he will put the sheep on His right, and the goats on the left. Then the King will say to those on His right, Come you who are blessed of My Father, inherit the kingdom prepared for you from the foundation of the world. For I was hungry and you gave me something to eat; I was thirsty and you gave me drink; I was a stranger, and you invited Me in; naked and you clothed Me; I was sick, and you visited Me; I was in prison, and you came to Me. Then the righteous will answer Him saying, Lord when did we see you hungry, and feed You, or thirsty, and give You drink? And when did we see You a stranger, and invite You in, or naked, and clothe You? And when did we see You sick, or in prison, and come to You?

> And the King will answer and say to them, Truly I say to you,
> to the extent that you did it to one of these brothers of Mine,
> even the least of them, you did it to Me [Matthew 25:31–40].

It is clear here that there can be no separation of the advancing of the kingdom of God from compassion, mercy, and justice. From this biblical foundation, we must move the church to initiatives of compassion, mercy, and justice. Compassion represents the love of God in us and flowing through us, and it creates our passion for lost people and the desire to see them experience new life. Mercy is our attitude toward broken people and broken communities. This is what gets us past the mind-set of blaming and judging people for where they are. Even when people are in bad situations because of their bad choices, mercy leads us to respond in a way that is beyond what they deserve. It is the way God looked on us through someone else when we were living lives away from God. This is why when God was calling the Israelites to extend justice to those around them, he reminded them that they used to be slaves. Our pride and judgment should be dismantled by remembering that God once delivered us from something. Truth be told, his grace and mercy are being poured out on us even now to deal with areas in our lives where we still struggle. This must be a part of our going out as a missional church.

Revitalizing the Church Through Evangelism and Justice

A missional approach to ministry could be the revitalizing strategy to turn a struggling church into a healthy one. When I see a struggling church, I wonder, *Has this church lost its passion for the surrounding community?* It's easy to lose touch, but it's not that hard to find out what is going on in your community and what is needed.

When I was serving as an associate pastor at a church in Minneapolis, some of our college students volunteered to study the needs of our community as part of a class project. Their work gave us a way of knowing what we needed to do. Schools or community centers in your community are also good places to start. Economic challenges have caused many public schools to cut their budgets, and typically after-school programs and extracurricular programs end up being sacrificed. Is there a need for a tutoring program in your community? Could your church provide a productive space for youth to come after school and do their homework?

Although I like the idea of using church building space for community outreach initiatives, I believe that getting out into the community is a better way for the church to be missional. So instead of bringing students to your church for tutoring, the church can send volunteers to a nearby school and maybe even start a program that is needed. The church could be missional just by stepping in and filling gaps in school programs. Many times this effort doesn't cost the church much money. In fact, time is usually the most significant sacrifice. When I was serving as an associate pastor, I was able to recruit retired teachers and business leaders to run initiatives such as a science and math program. The key is determine what the community needs, assess the resources and gifts of your church members, and then begin to mobilize for transformation.

Identifying the needs can also open up opportunities for advocacy, another way to give retired folks in our churches opportunities to make a difference. A lot of the meetings where decisions get made about schools, housing, and other areas of community development occur during the day. Having people from your church sit in on these meetings and then through forums come back and update the church on what's going on helps to deepen the connection between church and community. It also helps the church in understanding the systemic issues that are affecting the community, and it helps counteract that mind-set of rugged individualism.

Missional Church Planting

When a church is being planted, it's important to build in a missional culture from the start, for two important reasons: it lets those who are becoming part of the church know that reaching the community for kingdom advancement is a high priority, and it sends a message to the community that you will be more than simply a Sunday morning worship center. This is helpful especially when planting a church in an urban area, where there are often many church buildings. In fact, community leaders may question why another church is needed in the city. The reason they ask is that they see churches as buildings, not as a missional movement that will be a positive force for their community.

By serving and developing initiatives of justice right away, you gain credibility, which is a useful part of developing the right to share the gospel with people who don't know Christ. Serving and initiatives of justice also provide access to places in a community that evangelists can't go. You won't be invited into a public institution in a community to reach people for Christ, but you can gain access for the purpose of meeting needs and addressing the challenges the community faces. Pastors and other church leaders have to regularly show the congregation through scripture that this approach is part of advancing the kingdom.[1]

I have also been a part of evangelistic festivals that have come to cities with the goal of reaching the lost. For example, an evangelistic group will come into a metropolitan area and ask churches to help them raise $2 million or even more. Once the festival begins, though, it ends up looking more like a big party for church people. People do end up coming to the altar, the evangelistic group sends out a newsletter to its donors saying thousands of people became Christians, and we feel good that we have some sort of victory in our battle with Satan for lives. But what if $4 million had been raised, with half being used to bless the city and invested in churches where the festival was held? I offered this idea to one evangelistic organization, and it turned down my offer. I believe money invested to plant missional churches in a city is much more fruitful than festivals that don't have the capacity for follow-up to find out what kind of impact was really made. A holistic approach to kingdom advancement that includes justice requires much more than drop-in events. Justice ministry is relational, it takes time, and it is hard to describe well in a brochure. Yet the missional church as a planted and committed community can experience fruit over time.

When I was at the Sanctuary Covenant Church, I was privileged to see this kind of fruit in the form of changed lives. We started by getting out and taking the time to identify the needs in our community, and I tried not to let a Sunday go by without reminding the congregation that North Minneapolis was our community. The community thus became our focus and our mission field. We started a monthly event, Love Minneapolis, when we went into the community and served. Sometimes that meant bringing food to homeless people. Other times it meant picking up garbage or washing gang signs off the walls of a local business. We adopted schools in order to work with elementary and middle school students who were struggling with reading and doing math at grade level. We ran a workforce development initiative for adults in a community center. New families began to attend our Sunday morning worship. They came to church because we were meeting needs, and they sensed that we cared for them.

Extending the love of God is powerful. I used to say to our church staff that we couldn't guarantee that everyone we came in contact with in the church would become a Christian because we in fact don't save anybody. This is the work of God. But we can guarantee that we extend the love of Christ to everyone we come in contact with in the community.

Start by learning the needs of your community and understanding the gifts and abilities of the people in your church. Some churches recruit their members to serve as volunteers mainly within internal programs, but this keeps the church from a missional engagement of their community for transformation. When we better understand the need of our communities, we are able to invite our church members to pray and think of creative ways to meet those needs. Maybe there are retired people in the church waiting for the opportunity to make a difference in the lives of others and they can help develop the initiatives to do it.

Partnering with Other Ministries

Many of the issues facing communities in crisis are too big and complex for a single church to handle. Partnering with other churches or parachurches can enhance missional work. When I was youth pastor at Park Avenue United Methodist Church in Minneapolis, I was part of creating Urban Reclaim, an urban youth ministry. This was a network of youth pastors, parachurch leaders, community center directors, and public school support staff. Mainline churches, evangelical churches, Young Life, the YWCA, and local high schools were represented within this network.

We began by meeting monthly to support each other in the challenges of working with youth in underresourced communities. We also shared resources in order to develop initiatives in the community that none of us could do on our own. Our network grew to include public school and community center staff partners as well. Our missional approach gave us credibility in the community. Because of the relationships we developed, we had an open door to just about every public school and community center in the city. Because of our work, youth came to know Christ as their personal Savior and got the support they needed to get to college. We had discipleship initiatives and leadership development initiatives that taught character traits.

Just Do It

Some churches hesitate to get out in the community because they don't want to do the wrong thing and possibly cause more harm than good. Some refuse to go out into the community because of fear. Violence, problems that seem overwhelming, or a church's sense that it lacks adequate resources can keep the church from being missional. I say begin with prayer, and then let God move you to do something. Don't try to do it all, but do something. If that doesn't work, then pray again and then do something else. There is no excuse for any church not to be missional.

When we started at the Sanctuary, we would meet at our church offices for prayer and then go out into the community. We called these prayer walks. We weren't necessarily out there to lead someone to Christ, but if God wanted to do that, we were willing. We weren't out there to invite someone to our church, but if God wanted to do that, we were open. Our main focus was to experience the community and experience God. We came to learn that God was present in North Minneapolis way before we came on the scene. Your heart and mind change toward a community when you realize that no matter how tough the issues are, God is always there.

Mom's could do a prayer walk

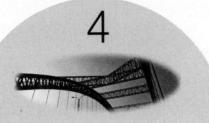

4

race

Within the first couple of years of the planting of the Sanctuary Covenant Church, we were experiencing pretty steady growth. But we wanted to make sure that we weren't just growing in numbers; we also wanted to develop as a reconciling community. Curtiss DeYoung, professor of reconciliation studies at Bethel University in St. Paul, Minnesota, and a longtime mentor and friend of mine, came and preached for us once on this important topic for the multi-ethnic and missional church. He challenged us during his sermon when he looked over our congregation and said, "I can see that you are a very diverse church. Praise God for this, but you still have a way to go in order to be a reconciling church." As he spoke, I felt both an affirmation and a challenge.

After that Sunday, we had some good discussion as a staff about what being a reconciling church means, and we knew that this had to be addressed in how we went about discipleship in our church. Our initiatives of discipleship were developed within the ministry area of one of our core values, equipping and formation—the area that focuses on spiritual growth and development. Our hope was that reconciliation would be linked to discipleship. Within this area we decided to launch a small groups ministry and would call these groups "community groups." Reconciliation would not be the sole focus of these groups, but by encouraging each group to be multi-ethnic, there would be a broader reconciling ethos among all of them.

I preached a sermon series, simply called, "Community," to set up the launching of our community groups ministry. I wanted the church to understand that the goal of our church shouldn't be just to become a diverse church, but to grow as a reconciling community that was dealing with the various walls that divide humanity. I pointed to scriptures on serving one another through love (Galatians 5:13) and bearing one another's burdens (Galatians 6:2). In a multi-ethnic and missional church, it's not enough to sit next to each other during a sermon, stand next to each other and sing worship songs, and park in the same parking lot. We had to be willing to do life together.

Using Stories of Race for Understanding

When we launched community groups in 2005, we asked people who were willing to be leaders to sign up for training. We would meet weekly for about eight weeks and then would have a larger all-church launch. It was during the training of leaders that something happened that we weren't totally prepared for.

Since we thought it was important for me to do some teaching with the leaders-in-training the first week, I decided that I would do a review of the vision, purpose, and core values of the church and then have a discussion on how they would connect to the initial studies that would take place within the community groups. As I was going over the core values of our church, I mentioned words such as *reconciliation, race, ethnicity*, and so forth. An older woman who happened to be European-American asked me why dealing with race was such a big deal: "Why do we have to talk about race so much in our church? Can't we just all be color-blind?" Then she paused for a moment and looked right at me with tears in her eyes: "My parents taught me that racism and prejudice are wrong. When I look at you, Pastor Efrem, I don't see race. I see the Holy Spirit that is within you. We are all God's children, and that's all that matters." I didn't want to respond too quickly because I knew that she meant well and was sincere in her remarks.

But before I could say something, another older woman, this one African-American, said, "Well, I don't know what you see when you look at me, but I'm a Black woman! Yes, the Holy Spirit is in me, but I'm Black, and I live in a world that reminds me daily that I'm Black, so I don't know what eyes you're using to look at people. And can't you see that Pastor Efrem is Black too?" Well, there it was: the elephant in the room had been exposed, and the tension was palpable. I had all kinds of conflicting thoughts running through my head at that moment. On one hand, I was excited because I knew how important this discussion was for moving from a diverse church to a reconciling church. At the same time, I wasn't sure where we would go from here. In fact, this is one of the reasons we don't have as many multi-ethnic and missional churches as we need in this nation. The homogeneous church is not without tension, but there is a greater sense of cultural comfort than there is in the post-Black, post-White church.

I responded to the tension by sharing my own stories of dealing with race, which I believe is a healthy approach to developing an authentic community. Many times the issue of race becomes contentious because we're not sharing our personal stories and listening to others' stories. Instead, we usually argue or silently live in the tension of issues surrounding race that are reflected in our polarized media. Or we carry around racial stereotypes or racial stories that are exaggerated. All of these reactions cause much harm in many cases and raise the dividing walls even higher.

Stories of Race in the Media

The stories of race we glean through the media especially concern me. These stories not only become volatile racial issues, but they become divided along conservative and liberal political lines. Hurricane Katrina, for example, became both a racial and a political issue. Many African-Americans looked at the way the local and federal government responded to the mostly African-American and poorer communities in New Orleans and didn't know how the images in the news reports could be viewed beyond race. The majority of faces stranded at the Superdome and shown on television were Black faces. The majority of families shown waiting for a bus and in some cases a boat to rescue them were Black. Add to that the tensions between the mayor of New Orleans, who was African-American, and the president of the United States at the time, who was European-American.

This was a dramatic storyline for the media that created and reflected much tension for an audience not as unified across racial lines as it should be. Rather than unifying the church around biblical compassion, mercy, and justice, the story of this hurricane became a way that some Christians became divided across issues of race. The tensions with Christians went even higher in some cases when the issue went from being just political and racial to being theological and racial. Some well-known White evangelical pastors proclaimed that Hurricane Katrina was God's judgment for the sins of America. Of course, that question led to more: If God wanted to judge America for its sins, why would he zero in on an urban city of the South? And why would he choose to destroy communities that would displace so many African-American families?

In 2008, we saw this matter of race at a new level in the presidential campaign that Barack Obama won. The campaign became a racial and political issue that caused both loudly voiced and silent tensions within the body of Christ. There was the tension around Obama's membership at Trinity United Church of Christ, led by well-known African-American pastor Jeremiah Wright. Many African-American evangelicals (I was one of them, though I don't agree with all of Wright's theology) were hurt by how a portion of one of his sermons was taken out of context by some conservatives for political reasons. The way this was done disrespected the Black church on many levels. In this same context, social justice and community organizing, both historic hallmarks of the Black church, were also made political by being called elements of a socialist and liberal agenda. I believe that many who took this position were so caught up in political ideology that they didn't realize the racial tensions that they were fueling. Many African-American and evangelical Christians knew it would be difficult to talk authentically with European-American evangelicals about this historic election.

There are as well issues that may not be either racial or political at their core but become both. For example, we could compare the way people perceive an African-American athlete being treated in the media versus the way a European-American athlete is treated. Two professional football players from Pennsylvania are an example. African-American quarterback Michael Vick of the Philadelphia Eagles went to prison for his connection to illegal dog fighting. Though he paid his debt to society and has since been a positive force both on and off the field, some in the media and some football fans continue to bring up the issue. Contrast this treatment to that of European-American quarterback Ben Roethilsberger of the Pittsburgh Steelers, who has been accused of sexual harassment multiple times as well as other negative off-the-field behavior. He was suspended for a few games, and no one has since paid any attention at all to his transgressions.

The issue could at its core be more about behavior than race, but the media make it both racial and political. If ESPN talks about it, it could become simply racial. If CNN picks up on the story, it then can become political as well. This is not to say that there aren't issues of racial discrimination and prejudice in sports or any other field. But in either case, issues of race become tense when we're talking about them in the context of something we saw on television or something we heard someone else say about an issue connected in some way to race. Without diminishing the impact or influence of race in our society, I'm trying to get at how to deal with race in a way that ultimately brings about harmony, unity, and common mission within the church and the broader society. If this is the goal, then you don't start by talking about the hot-button racial and political issues of the day. I'm not saying you never talk about them; I'm just suggesting that you don't start there. I suggest you start with your own personal stories in the context of race and then prepare to listen, without quick judgment, to the stories of others.

My Own Stories

After the two women in that training circle for community group leaders spoke up, I began to share my own stories. I started with the stories of my parents and grandparents. My father, Force Smith, is from Monroe, Louisiana. He was raised on a cotton farm where he rode horses and milked cows and picked cotton. He lived on the Black side of the railroad tracks, grew up in the Jim Crow segregation of the South, and went to all-Black schools. He called White men "Sir" and White women "Ma'am," but he never heard White people pay that same respect to adult Blacks. When my dad became an adult, he left the segregated South and headed up North looking for job opportunities. He eventually made it to Minneapolis, Minnesota, where he met and married my mother, Sandra Knight, who was originally from Birmingham, Alabama, but had moved to Minnesota with my grandmother and three other siblings when she was a child. She too was born in the segregated South of Jim Crow, but by the time she was in high school in Minneapolis, she was experiencing the integrated public school culture of the Midwest.

My parents shared many stories with me about their upbringing in the segregated South and remember vividly the days of the civil rights movement. My parents thought it was important for my younger brother, Tramaine, and me to know our grandparents and other relatives in the South and understand the world in which they grew up, so we spent many summers in the South when we were young. At first I hated what I viewed as forced exile because I wanted to spend the summers with my neighborhood and school friends, but soon I came to appreciate this experience, and as an adult now, I truly appreciate those experiences, which guided me to become a leader of multi-ethnic and missional ministry.

Although I spent summers in the South some time after the civil rights movement, the racial climate in Louisiana was different from that in Minnesota. It wasn't the overt racism of cross burnings, colored-only sections, and segregated schools. It was more a sustained sense of Blacks and White having and knowing their place in society. I remember when a young White man came to my grandparents' house one day to check the gas meter. He couldn't have been older than his mid-twenties. The whole time he was there, my grandmother called this young man by his last name or "Sir," while he called my grandmother by her first name. I thought this young man was being quite disrespectful by addressing my grandmother in this way, but I was a child and so just watched and remained silent. This was one of the ways of the South at the time, and I would learn more of them. I learned, when we went into town, to make sure that I said "Ma'am" and "Sir" when talking to White adults, though it was something I didn't think too much about in addressing Whites in Minnesota. I was certainly polite and respectful to them, but in Louisiana, the way of addressing White people seemed to me to be about a person's place in society.

When my brother and I returned to Minnesota, I talked to my mother and father about my observations and asked questions because I was a curious and talkative child. This is what led my parents to share their own stories of race. Because of the love and our close relationship, it's as if their stories became mine, as if I too were carrying them. That's true for all of us, even when the stories are racist or are full of unresolved anger or hurt toward people of other races. Those stories, good and bad, affect us. For some of us, our journey around race may begin by realizing both the positive and negative ways that our race stories bear on the views we have today.

I'm fortunate that my parents don't live in anger or hurt from these stories of their experiences as people of color. Rather, they used the stories to help me and my siblings navigate this racialized world as change agents. Now that I am an adult, I have my own race stories as well.

Here's one. One Sunday evening I was driving in my car with two other African-American men from church to go to the store to get some ice, sodas, and dessert for our dinner together. Both are college educated, work in the corporate world, own their own homes, and are married with children. As we were about to pull into the parking lot of the store, I saw flashing lights in my rearview mirror. I wasn't speeding. Two White police officers approached the car, one with his hand visibly on his gun holster. As the other officer came to my side of the car, I rolled down my window. "Let me see everyone's identification in this car," he demanded.

I was surprised because it made sense that he would ask for my driver's license and registration, but it didn't make sense to me that he needed to see everyone else's identification. Before I could say something, one of the guys in the car with me said, "We better just do what he says." We all handed the officer our identifications and waited for over twenty minutes. Eventually the officer came back to the car, gave us each our identifications, and told us we could go. He gave no explanation about why we were stopped. And this isn't the only time this kind of thing has happened to me.

In another instance, I was sitting on my flight in first class waiting to take off. It was a late flight, and I was tired and hungry, looking forward to a meal on the plane. Normally I would have bought something in the airport, but since I knew I would be in first class, I saved the high cost of an airport dinner. The only other person in first class was an older woman who was White. As I settled into my seat, the flight attendant, White and female, walked over to me and asked me if I was sitting in the right seat. I said that I was and noticed that she didn't ask the other passenger the same question. Once we were in the air, the flight attendant served a meal to the older White woman but never served me. When I pushed my call button, she came over to me and said, "I'm so sorry. I forgot that you were sitting here. Would you like something to eat?" I must confess that I was so offended and upset that I turned down the meal. I'm in no way saying this was the right response and I sure was hungry that whole flight. As I look back on it now, I wonder if the flight attendant just professionally didn't do a good job of serving me in general on the plane that evening. But because I wasn't served well, in contrast to the White woman who was served well, it becomes challenging to not see this as an issue of race on some level.

As I shared stories like these with the community group leaders at the Sanctuary, there were gasps, tears, and looks of shock from many of the Whites in the circle. The Blacks and some of the other people of color looked as if they were reliving their own stories as I told mine. There were some Whites there that evening who were further along in their journeys around race and offered gracious comments. The White woman whose remarks led us into this conversation said with more tears flowing down her cheeks, "I'm so sorry. I didn't know this type of stuff still happened." Her husband wanted to write a letter on my behalf to the airline. I also realized that some of the people of other ethnicities in the room had looks on their faces that led me to believe they were feeling left out of what had become a mostly Black and White conversation. I acknowledged that and invited a Hispanic brother to share his stories.

Inclusiveness and recognition are healthy ways of dealing with the issue of race in a multi-ethnic and missional church. We begin to create the beloved community by sharing our stories and listening to one another. I'm not saying that we were always great at this at the Sanctuary. On many occasions in staff meetings, elder board meetings, and other gatherings, we misunderstood each other, made judgmental statements, and hurt one another. Sometimes my own comments caused offense and the pain, and I learned the importance of seeking forgiveness. At one point we even brought in a group of reconciliation facilitators to assist our leaders in having prayerful, healthy, and authentic dialogue around issues of race.

Systemic Issues of Race

The stories we shared that evening for the most part were personal ones of race, and most of them came from those in the room who were non-White. We didn't get into the even larger systemic issues of race that surrounded us in the Twin Cities of Minneapolis and Saint Paul, Minnesota, but that soon changed. In 2005 the Brookings Institute did a study of the disparities that existed in the Twin Cities across race, class, and place. Some of the members of our church who were executives in both for-profit and nonprofit organizations were involved in parts of the process. The study found that some groups were not enjoying the same levels of prosperity as others:

- The Twin Cities region has the twelfth highest college attainment rate among the one hundred largest metropolitan areas: 33 percent of its residents have a bachelor's degree or higher. However, only 19 percent of African-Americans, 11 percent of Mexicans, and 8 percent of Hmong do.
- The region has the fourteenth highest median household income among the largest metropolitan areas. In 2000, Whites had a median household income of $56,642, while the typical household income for African-Americans lagged at $29,404 and $38,909 for Mexicans.
- The Twin Cities boasts one of the highest homeownership rates in the country—ranked seventh, in fact—a strong sign of wealth building among families. In 2000, 76 percent of Whites were home owners in 2000, while only 32 percent of Blacks owned homes.
- The region's overall poverty ranks among the lowest in the country, yet poverty still disproportionately plagues some segments of the population. In 2000, only 4 percent of Whites were poor, but one-third of all Hmong lived below the federal poverty line.[1]

How to Address Issues of Race

We cannot ignore the issue and the impact of race within the multi-ethnic and missional church. We have to deal with the issues surrounding race so that the post-Black, post-White church can be a healthy and reconciling church. So outside of sharing and listening to personal stories around race, there are other ways to address the issue. One is to define terms around race so everyone uses a common language, which can lead to unity. One of the reasons post-Black, post-White churches are hard to develop and sustain is that there so many definitions around race and racism. For example, theologian John Piper defines *racism* as "an explicit or implicit belief or practice that qualitatively distinguishes or values one race over other races."[2] I believe this definition points us in the right direction but falls somewhat short in that it makes racism an individual and internalized feeling of prejudice that can lead to the devaluing of a group of people simply because of their race.

I believe this definition is better: *racism* is prejudice plus power used to discriminate or oppress a group of people solely because of their race. I came to this definition through the writings on racism and White privilege by pastor and multicultural ministry leader Joseph Barndt:

> Racism is clearly more than simple prejudice or bigotry. Everyone is prejudiced, but not everyone is racist. To be prejudiced means to have opinions, even after contrary facts are known. To be racially prejudiced means to have distorted opinions about people of other races. Racism goes beyond prejudice. It is backed up by power. Racism is the power to enforce one's prejudice. More simply stated, racism is prejudice plus power.[3]

With this definition, it is important as we share and listen to the stories of others that we recognize that racism affects us both individually and in broader systemic ways. On one level, we can dismantle racism through our individual relationships across race and through our daily choices. Individually we can decide to speak out against a racist joke, and we can individually expose stereotypes of an entire group of people.

These individual acts do make a difference, but systemic racism takes more than individual acts. This type of racism must be dealt with by groups of people reimagining and working to redefine communities, institutions, and other structures. It takes more than one individual in most cases to change a school system, a corporation, or a political system. Martin Luther King Jr. didn't bring about change through the civil rights movement all by himself. We must remember Fannie Lou Hammer, Ralph Abernathy, John Lewis, and Rosa Parks. There are also Catholics, Protestants, and Orthodox Jews whom we don't know who also worked for change. People of various ethnicities opened up churches, community centers, and homes. This is why multiple multi-ethnic and missional churches are needed. This is why I speak not of just individuals but of churches, and not just of churches but a movement.

A Deeper Understanding of Race

In the post-Black, post-White church, race cannot be a topic to skirt around. It must instead be engaged for the church to grow in its capacity to be missional.

A healthy discussion on race that assists in the development of a healthy multi-ethnic and missional church begins by dealing with race as a way of identifying human beings. Any discussion on race has to deal with an evil that can come out of living in a racialized society, and that is racism. Some would argue that the primary product of a racialized society is racism. What can be agreed on is that racism is an evil that leads to unhealthy and destructive outcomes. With this in mind, it is essential to define racism so that it might be clearly revealed for what it is and be dismantled.

Let's dive deeper into this issue by presenting some definitions that can provide clarity. Race is about categorizing and valuing a people based on skin color and other physical features. It ultimately is an artificial social structure that places the White group on top, the Black group on the bottom, and the Yellow, Red, and Brown groups in the middle. There doesn't seem to be any serious biological evidence to support race, however. Differences in skin color and physical features alone are not enough to separate people into classified race groups. Nevertheless, people have been placed in these groups, which are associated with levels of emotion, intellect, and, in the case of slavery in the early history of the United States, the question of the full humanity of Africans. The writing of Christian sociologist George A. Yancey has been helpful in my thinking about race in this way:

> The criteria that our society uses to categorize us in separate races are not derived through a logical study of nature. If racial distinctions do not occur as a natural phenomenon then how did they develop? Part of the answer is the fact that this concept of race is what we sociologists call a social construct. It is something that society has developed on its own apart from the natural reality that surrounds society. In short, we made it up. Over time we decided that this group of people should be of one race and that another group of people should be of a different race. We developed rules of segregation to control the mixing of races. Eventually we actually began to believe that this separation is part of the natural order of things. Some of us Christians may even believe that God ordered the separation. All the while we forget that this is something we have made up.[4]

But even though race is made up, it has an important impact and implications in our racialized society. You have to look at it like the unreal world in the movie *The Matrix*. The storyline of the popular science fiction trilogy that captured many moviegoers some years ago takes place after a war between machines and human beings. The technology and innovation that humankind made up now enslave it. The machines create a false world for the enslaved humans known in the movie as the Matrix. Although the Matrix was a computer-generated world, it was real to the human beings plugged into it. It was the only world they knew, and they couldn't imagine any other. But some humans escaped their enslavement and lived in the real world, a city known as Zion. They went back and forth between Zion and the Matrix to save those enslaved in it.

In the same way, race is an artificial, human-created social construct. It is the machine that has taken us over and created a false reality. Even the people who don't think race is an issue are led to believe race is real based on how they've been conditioned. Blacks recognize race as an issue too much, and many Whites recognize it too little or not at all. So in a racialized society, a Black person may attribute every negative experience to race, whereas a White person may have a series of negative experiences that he or she never attributes to race. This is due to how race categorizes a people. If you're at the top, you don't have to think about yourself as part of a racial group. When you're in the middle, maybe it's an issue from time to time. If you're on the bottom, it's an issue too much of the time. There is somewhat of an out to this if you're in the middle or the bottom, but it's not necessarily a healthy one. That option is assimilation. If you assimilate into the value system and practices of White culture, race can feel like less of an issue to you. But if race becomes an issue, it can be shocking and surprising. You exclaim, "I can't believe this is happening to me!"

Assimilation into the values of the dominant culture helps Whiteness become a neutral culture and not a race at all. This is at the core of White privilege. The dominant culture has the power to decide and sustain what is neutral and natural. This is not to say that all of what makes up White culture is bad, but placing it at the core gives it a higher value than the culture of other groups. This concept of race helps to sustain false identities and structures. This is why we need liberation from the race matrix. We need to deal not only with racism but with the construct of race itself. There is another way of living outside the labels, structures, and behaviors of race.

The other way, the better way, is to dismantle the structure of race by finding new identity as Christians. This is why true transformation and reconciliation can be found in the post-Black, post-White church. Our belief in the centrality and authority of scripture ought to lead us to see God's true design and desire for human beings. The scriptures show us that God didn't create human beings within categories of race that place one group of people over another. In *The Matrix*, the central character, Neo, was offered a pill that would show him the truth and provide him the understanding of his new identity. The "pill" for our escape from living primarily in racial identities is the Word of God, the Bible:

> Then God said, "Let the waters teem with swarms of living creatures, and let birds fly above the earth in the open expanse of the heavens." And God created the great sea monsters, and every living creature that moves, with which the waters swarmed after their kind, and every winged bird after its kind; and God saw that it was good. And God blessed them, saying "Be fruitful and multiply, and fill the waters in the seas, and let the birds multiply on the earth." And there was evening and there was morning, a fifth day. Then God said, "Let the earth bring forth living creatures after their kind: cattle and creeping things and beast of the earth after their kind"; and it was so. And God made the beasts of the earth after their kind, and the cattle after their kind, and everything that creeps on the ground after its kind; and God saw that it was good. Then God said, "Let Us make man in Our image, according to Our likeness; and let them rule over the fish of the sea and over the birds of the sky and over the cattle and over every creeping thing that creeps on the earth. And God created man in His own image, in the image of God He created him; male and female He created them" [Genesis 1:20–27].

When God created the animals, he created them after their "own kind." They were created in groups and were to be fruitful and multiply in those groups. This is why in the animal kingdom, you would never see an elephant and a hippopotamus come together to create offspring. You are not going to see "hippo-phants" from such a union because God created the animals to multiply among their own kind. God did not create humans this way. We are created as one human race in God's own image. God did not create human beings in categories of separate races or place a higher value on some and a lower value on others. When we live divided by racial categories and characteristics, we live as the creatures that we are supposed to have dominion over. We do not live up to our identity as beings made in the image of God and our true identity from our creator. Race is not God's original intention for humanity.

So how did race come to be in the first place and have the tremendous impact that it does? We can conclude only that race is a part of the after-effects of the story of the fall of Adam and Eve. Race is a part of the matrix of a fallen and sin-filled world. God created us all equal, as one people with an identity found in being in his image. Race takes away that equality and identity and becomes an idol that prevents us from living in God's image and thus from being in intimate relationship with God. How can we discover day by day what it means to be in God's image and not be in relationship with God? To live by racial categories is to find identity and life apart from God.

It's not just that racism is a sin; rather, the entire structure of race points to false identities within fallen humanity. Race has such an impact on us because it is a spiritual force. It must be dismantled by truth and by new identity found in Christ and in the indwelling of the Holy Spirit. Part of the dismantling comes with forging the post-Black, post-White church. Through this beloved Christ-centered community, we can live collectively through the power of the Holy Spirit, dying to the old identities of race labels and into the new identities of being God's beloved children.

In my book, *Jump: Into a Life of Further and Higher*, I deal with this important connection between what I call the beloved life and the beloved community.[5] We find new identity beyond racial identity in Christ. This does not mean that the post-Black, post-White church delivers us from the matrix of a racialized society altogether. We are still in the world, yet through new identity, we are also otherworldly. Race will continue to be an issue until Jesus comes back and we live in the community of God's new heaven and the new earth. Until then, the multi-ethnic and missional church can provide a sneak preview of what that eternal kingdom looks like. We can live into the new identities of our citizenship in that kingdom right now.

The alternative is the reality of what the segregated church looks like now. In the segregated church, we proclaim our new identity and new life in Christ, but we live within the system of the old and false identities of this world. To this extent, we are in the world and of the world. By desiring the homogeneous church, we actually desire racial hedonism. Why not practice now living into the new kingdom community where we will live eternally?

This concept of our identity in Christ is key to moving beyond the matrix of race. Matthew 1 tells us about Christ's human genealogy, as a descendent of Abraham: "To Abraham was born Isaac; and to Isaac, Jacob; and to Jacob, Judah and his brothers; and to Judah were born Perez and Zerah by Tamar" (Matthew 1:1–3).

This is the earthly family tree of Jesus. Could it be that there is a connection between the bloodline of Jesus and the bloodshed on Calvary that washes away our sin and brings about both eternal life and new life right now? This genealogy of Jesus shows us the significance of him as the Son of man. Jesus is part of the family of Abraham and Isaac, but he is also the Son of God. His heritage ultimately begins before the beginning of time. It is before and beyond this earthly realm. Before the creation of the heavens and the earth, he is. As the Gospel of John says, "In the beginning was the Word, and the Word was with God, and the Word was God. He was in the beginning with God. All things came into being by Him, and apart from Him nothing came into being that has come into being. In Him was life and the life was the light of men. . . . And the Word became flesh, and dwelt among us, and we beheld His glory as of the only begotten from the Father, full of grace and truth" (John 1:14).

The Multi-Ethnicity of Jesus

That Jesus is the Son of man is empowering to us because we live in him and he in us. As a descendent of Abraham, to whom God promises his role as the father of nations, Jesus is heir to great multi-ethnic diversity. This is important to note in connection to his human family tree and his identity as the Son of man. Could this be Jesus, Son of multi-ethnic hu(man)ity?

When we look through scripture, we see the interplay of ethnicity and the way race came to be and see how Jesus is the fruit of a long and diverse bloodline. A woman named Tamar listed in the genealogy of Jesus provides some insight into his multi-ethnic and multicultural family tree. We learn about her in Genesis 38. As a Canaanite, Tamar is the descendent of Canaan, who had been cursed by his grandfather, Noah. For a time in our Christian culture, there was a theology accepted in order to justify slavery within the United States that the Canaanite was Black. This type of racial theology was helped to reinforce the false and inferior identity of Blackness. Biblical scholar J. Daniel Hays sheds light on this issue:

> It may also be pertinent to note that the Canaanites are ethnically very close to the Israelites . . . the Canaanite language and culture is similar to that of the Israelites. They were also probably very similar in appearance. The critical difference was in regard to the gods that they worshipped. So . . . the curse on Canaan has absolutely nothing to do with Black Africa. Furthermore, because of the close ethnic affinity between the Canaanites and the Israelites, it can be said that this curse has nothing to do with race at all.[6]

Note that Canaan and his family are the original inhabitants of Israel and Palestine. Canaan's brother, Cush, and his family are the original inhabitants of Ethiopia and the Sudan. Another brother, Mizraim, and his family are the original inhabitants of Egypt. And yet another brother, Phut, and his family are the original inhabitants of Libya. Canaan's uncle, Japheth, has a group of descendents (including Ruth) who are known as the Moabites, whom some scholars believe are the ancestors of Europeans. This means that Jesus's bloodline has Israelis, Palestinians, Ethiopians, Sudanese, Egyptians, Libyans, and various European ethnic groups in it.

The biblical world of Jesus thus spans Africa, Asia, and Europe, which means that Jesus walked the earth as a multi-ethnic human being, not as Black or White. None of these ancestors dominated his identity, unlike the days of slavery in the United States when a person who was even one-eighth Black (which amounted to a teaspoon of Black blood) was classified as Black. If this race rule were applied to Jesus, he would have been considered Black. But race rules don't apply in scripture or in the kingdom of God. Jesus both transcends and dismantles race. The fact that he was multi-ethnic as a human being is significant.

When Jesus was hanging on the cross and the blood was dripping from his head, hands, and feet, that was multi-ethnic blood. When we say that Jesus died for all of our sins, that is true both figuratively and literally because all humanity was pumping through him and pouring out of him. He was the sacrificial lamb of all of sinful humanity and therefore embodies all of humanity in both the carrying and shedding of this precious blood. This truly is in this sense a substitutionary death. That is why the multi-ethnic and missional church must find identity in the multi-ethnic Jesus who is the Son of man and the Son of God. Through the Holy Spirit, this multi-ethnic Jesus lives in us. In him is new life and new identity.

Ethnicity and Tribes

Although race is not biblical, ethnicity is. We see groups of people described by ethnicity, nationality, and tribe within the scriptures. We also see where some of the same dynamics that take place in our racialized world also come into play in the social structures of the Bible, for example, in the ethnic divide between Jew and Gentile. Other social divides connect more directly to social divides of our own day, such as class and gender. But we see through scripture that these divides are dealt with in Christ, as Paul tells the Galatians: "There is neither Jew nor Greek, there is neither slave nor free man, there is neither male nor female; for you are all one in Christ Jesus" (Galatians 3:28).

As Jesus is walking the earth, we see him dealing head-on with the divisions within the social structures of his day. He sits at the well with a Samaritan woman (John 4); heals the daughter of a Canaanite woman (Luke); and sits at table with a tax collector and immediately after is touched by a hemorrhaging woman while he is in the midst of a large crowd (Matthew 9). The multi-ethnic Jesus deals with the social structures and divides of his day and connects them both to the kingdom that he proclaims and the cross on which he will hang. Christ brings unity into divided humanity by offering new life. His miraculous works are the signs of what potentially can happen through the power, authority, and transformation found in him. In Christ Jesus, we are no longer red, yellow, brown, black, and white. We are new creatures in him. We are freed from false identities, but we retain the gift of our true identities of ethnicity and nationality. Although these characteristics are biblical, they can become false identities when we live them outside our relationship with God through Jesus Christ and the indwelling of the Holy Spirit. This means we never put our ethnicity or nationality above our identity in Christ.

This hierarchy of identity can be problematic for people who have made being Christian synonymous with being American. What does my identity in Christ mean for my relationship with another Christian in, say, South Africa? Am I closer in relationship eternally with another American or another Christian who is a citizen of another nation? Our nationality can become a base of worldly pride, our ethnicity can lead to ethnocentrism, and our tribalism can cause civil war. But our ethnicities, nationalities, and tribes in Christ can become a vehicle to give God glory and advance his kingdom in the world. This new identity in Christ is what makes the multi-ethnic church both healthy and missional. This healthy, beloved community is better positioned to fulfill the Great Commission both locally and globally.

The biblically based theology of race in the post-Black, post-White church must show up in teaching, preaching, and other initiatives of Christian formation. For many, dismantling old identities of race in order to live into the new identity of Christ-centered multi-ethnicity will be like a second conversion. This process is a journey. I remember how sometimes people at the Sanctuary Covenant Church would think that a sermon series on race would be too long, even if the sermons were full of scripture. And some would say, "When are we going to get off this race issue and focus on Jesus again in the sermons?"

The issue for many people is that because of all the uncomfortable feelings that arise around of race, they would prefer a quicker process. Many suffer from what I call "race fatigue": they want to deal with race quickly and get it over with so that we can move on to easier issues. In some cases, this has to do with a fear of living in sustained guilt. I've been to some Christian seminars dealing with race, and they have felt like White guilt sessions. I wondered why I was even in the room because it was so much about Whites as the guilty party. Nevertheless, I realize that truly dealing with and dismantling the false identities of race require dealing with White privilege, individual and structural racism, and oppression. But any Christian approach to dealing with race should be full of grace. We also need to remember that we all carry the issues and baggage of the sin of race and racism. This is why prayerful, authentic, and ongoing dialogue about race is so important.

Beyond dialogue and a biblical theology, we must find other ways to facilitate learning and awareness that lead to competencies and skills that will equip us to feel more comfortable in tackling the issue of race and empower us for multi-ethnic ministry. The more we know about the impact of race historically and today, the better chance we have at forging a new future as the beloved community.

Raising Cross-Cultural Awareness and Racial Understanding

I'm fortunate to be part of a denomination that offers many opportunities for pastors, lay leaders, and church members to grow in the cross-cultural awareness and racial understanding. Through the Department of Compassion, Mercy, and Justice, as well as within regional conferences, the Evangelical Covenant church offers several initiatives. One is an invitation to racial righteousness, an experience that challenges participants to move beyond language and knowledge of racial righteousness to a deeper place of personal awareness, responsibility, healing, and action. Participants are equipped to engage in relationship- and community-building activities to move toward true community across ethnic and racial lines, explore racial and ethnic injustices that exist in our society, and identify action steps for change, both personally and as a community.[7]

Racial Righteousness

Racial righteousness is an experience that points to the ability to live as the righteous and beloved children of God in a world where race matters. Facilitators of different ethnicities are trained in pairs and go on site to a local church. The program usually begins with a meal on Friday evening, continues all day Saturday, and concludes with worship on Sunday morning. This provides an entire weekend of focus for a congregation. Smaller congregations can include the whole church in this initiative. Medium to larger churches have to select or have sign-ups for smaller groups to participate. Because the Sanctuary Covenant Church grew to become a church of close to a thousand, we initially did this initiative every year for three years. I participated in it twice and found it to be very helpful in providing unifying definitions of key terms so that we could have a common language for talking about race.

Through readings, videos, and presentations by the facilitators, we gained a deeper understanding of the impact of race historically and today. It was a truly multi-ethnic experience that took the issue of race and ethnicity beyond a Black and White conversation. Asian, Hispanic, and Native American perspectives and stories were shared throughout the experience. There was a good mix of large and small group activities so that everyone had a chance to ask clarifying questions and share how they were feeling throughout the experience. At the end of the day on Saturday, we collectively developed a church covenant for dealing with issues of race and creating a strategy for congregational unity. A number of churches within the conference where I serve now have gone through this initiative and found it very fruitful. A member of one of our churches had this comment about the experience:

> What's next? My personal goal is to raise the level of dialogue and ultimately the level of individual, corporate, and systemic commitment to the young people with whom I have contact. I want to hear more of their stories. No, not hear, but really listen to what they have to say. By respecting and valuing their personal narratives, I can validate them and create a foundation

of trust so that they will hear and listen to my story. Both generations learn from each other. To break the chains of indifference, racism, bigotry, and other negative situations is humanly impossible. In Christ, with the power of the Holy Spirit, all things are possible.

Sankofa

Another Evangelical Covenant program is Sankofa, an African word for a depiction of a bird with its head pointing back at its tail. This depiction is stating that you have to be willing to look back in order to go forward.

Sanofa is a four-day bus ride that begins in Chicago and makes its way to Birmingham, Alabama. Participants are paired across race and ethnicity in order to process the experience throughout the journey. On the bus, videos are shown that deal with the historic divide of race in America. Though other ethnic stories may be shared, there is a primary focus on the Black and White divide. Stops are made on the way down south and back at historic sites that are part of the racial story. Ending in Birmingham is of great significance because it is the home of the Civil Rights Museum. The facilitator for the journey provides discussion questions and topics for each of the pairs to work through in order to gain deeper understanding and begin to think through the development of new ministries of compassion, mercy, and justice within their local churches.

Journey 2 Mosaic

Two of the other conferences within the Evangelical Covenant church thought it was important to develop their own bus journeys similar to the Sankofa journey yet unique to the cultural context of their regions of the country. From this the Journey 2 Mosaic (J2M) initiatives were born. J2M began in the Pacific Southwest Conference, where I now serve. It is facilitated by Greg Yee, who is Chinese-American and serves as the associate superintendent of the conference, and Walter Contreras, who is Hispanic and serves as the director of outreach and Hispanic church planting.

With their cultural experiences and insight, we developed a journey that went beyond the Black and White story and told the unique narrative of the western United States. J2M begins in Oakland, California, which has important yet mostly untold stories of African-Americans. Participants of J2M begin by going on the Black Panthers legacy tour in Oakland. I had perceived the Black Panthers to be both a militant and renegade group who were the violent alternative to the civil rights movement. But the tour showed me a different side to the Black Panthers. They pioneered feeding programs, including free breakfast and free lunch programs. We see the fruit of these initiatives through free lunch programs for low-income children in public schools today. The Black Panthers also worked to lower crime in the Black communities of major cities and started multiple Black-owned businesses to spearhead economic development enterprises. As I took in all of this new information during the tour, I couldn't help thinking, "If I'm African-American and needed to have my former views changed on this aspect of African-American history, how many people of other ethnicities have even more misperceptions of African-Americans?"

The second day we rode the bus to the Central Valley of California to experience one aspect of the Hispanic story. Like the Sankofa journey, we watched videos on the bus to increase our awareness of various issues of race and racism. In the Central Valley, we spent the day with migrant workers and learning from a Hispanic pastor about immigration (from a perspective that I believe the church needs to hear more).

One the third day, our bus took us to Los Angeles. At our first stop, the National Japanese Museum, we learned about Japanese internment camps in California during World War II. Because my experiences around race had been mostly limited to Black and

White, this journey was particularly meaningful to me, and it raised even further my cross-cultural awareness. After each experience, we came together as group for a debriefing circle, in which one of us would share a devotional; we would then share how we were feeling and have a time of prayer. This helped to focus us on the bigger outcome throughout the journey.

On the evening of the third day, we went to the Fred Jordan Mission in downtown Los Angeles on Skid Row, where there is a significant concentration of homelessness and poverty. Led by the Fred Jordan staff, we talked about homelessness and poverty and then went out into streets. We brought bread, bottled water, and an invitation to the programs at the Fred Jordan Mission. We prayed with people, but most important, we were ministered to. We met God on the streets of Skid Row. The group spent the night at the Fred Jordan Mission. The next morning, before heading back to Northern California, we worshipped at a multi-ethnic Covenant church in Long Beach.

Conclusion

Dealing with issues of race and racism is not easy, but it is needed if we hope to move from simply a diverse congregation to a beloved community. We must be willing to share our stories and listen to the stories of others. We must have a biblically rooted theology of race. We also need ongoing initiatives that raise our awareness and develop competencies that bring us out of the discomfort of boldly dealing with race so that we can dismantle racial barriers and live in new identities of righteousness. This is slow, hard, and sometimes painful work. But if we are willing to stay on the journey, blessings await us, especially the blessing of living in an earthly community that points toward the new community where we will live eternally.

5

the gift of the black church

'm a regional leader in a predominantly European-American and evangelical denomination; nevertheless, the Black church is in me. Being African-American doesn't automatically mean the Black church is in you. You have to be in the Black church before the Black church can truly be in you. I was raised in the Black church and influenced by its experience of worship. When I preach, it's obvious that the Black church is in me, and when I sing, the Black church is flowing out of me.

I'm also influenced by the historic social action and community development of the Black church. This historic influence was evident during slavery, Jim Crow, the civil rights movement, and through many faith-based community development and advocacy initiatives today. I'm also influenced by the theologies and ministries practices of the Black church as well. Both the Black liberation theology of James Cone and the reconciliation theologies of Howard Thurman, Martin Luther King Jr., and John Perkins are burning bushes within my soul: they play critical roles in my sense of calling and ministry purpose. Unique shepherding practices shape how I do hospital visits, officiate the sacraments, and provide biblical counsel to families and individuals. I love and honor the Black church, which taught me how to preach, how to be a community leader, how to be sensitive to the moving of the Holy Spirit, how to love sinners, how to fight for biblical kingdom justice, and how to forgive my so-called enemies. For this and more, I love the Black church.

If that's the case, you might ask, "How can you be so passionate about the post-Black, post-White church and have so much Black church in you? How can you be so committed to the multi-ethnic and missional church and the Black church simultaneously?" My answer is that the multi-ethnic and missional church is a healthy church when its members bring their unique ethnic and cultural gifts and experiences and share them with others to the glory of God. To this extent, their unique gifts become a gift to the broader body of Christ followers.

When I served as senior pastor of the Sanctuary Covenant Church, I learned over time that I would do the congregation a disservice if I didn't bring my unique cultural gifts and experiences into the church. I went from trying to be all things to all people (particularly the predominantly European-Americans in the congregation) to understanding my unique gifts and bringing them to bear in this setting. I felt internal pressure to connect to this majority group within the experience of worship. This was nothing new to me. Having grown up in Minnesota, I had spent my whole life thus far having to communicate in predominantly White settings. At some point, we African-Americans and other people of color have to learn how to communicate to and within the dominant culture.

This was the task before me in the first year of preaching Sunday after Sunday at the Sanctuary. I came into this position doubting that I could communicate effectively as a Black preacher, so I began to study those I had come to know as solid White preachers. Some preach sitting on a stool, with their Bible and notes on a music stand. Others have used movie clips to introduce their sermons, so I began to implement these styles at the Sanctuary. But when I was invited to preach at a Black church, I went back to the style I was raised in. One Sunday afternoon after I had preached at a Black church, a European-American woman who was a member of the Sanctuary came up to me and said, "I wish you would preach like that at the Sanctuary. You seemed so free and passionate about the Word of God!" That's when I saw that European-Americans weren't coming to the Sanctuary to hear a Black preacher preach to them as if he were White. They were coming for a truly authentic multi-ethnic experience.

I realized at that moment that for the church to be authentic to its vision and purpose, I had to preach and lead from the unique place and context in which God created and developed me. God had developed me for missional impact through a specific cultural context of ministry. Now I needed to share the gifts within me out of that experience with the community at the Sanctuary, and the gifts I had to share come from the Black church.

The Development of the Black Church

The origins of the Black church can be traced back to slavery, and specifically the slave owners' view of their African slaves. In their history of the Black church, Anne Pinn and Anthony Pinn write:

> With the growth in the population of enslaved Africans in North
> America during the 1600s came an increase in laws designed
> to tightly control the behavior of slaves. These laws made it
> clear that enslaved Africans were regarded as property for life
> and throughout all generations. Understanding themselves

to be civilized, Europeans reasoned that Africans must be uncivilized. . . . This commonly held attitude helped Europeans justify the enslavement of Africans because Europeans did not consider themselves to be harming fellow human beings but merely capturing and working beasts of burden.[1]

European Christian slave owners used the story of Noah cursing his grandson Canaan (Genesis 9; see Chapter Three) as biblical justification for their view and treatment of African slaves, although some Christian groups, such as the Quakers and Puritans, worked toward the spiritual conversion of Africans. But in many cases, the Christian doctrine shared with Africans who converted still supported the institution of slavery. This was especially the case early on with the Puritans. The Black church formed as African slaves begin to read the scriptures and understand Christianity for themselves. Pinn and Pinn continue:

> Enslaved Africans recognized the contradiction between word and deed, and those who still embraced the Christian tradition moved beyond falsehoods and hypocrisy. They made the Gospel of Christ a liberating religious experience by dropping the message of docility and instead understanding the Christian life as a free existence. Those enslaved Africans who sought to shape the Christian faith in ways that responded to their existential condition and spiritual needs developed what is known as the invisible institution. The invisible institution refers to secret religious meetings held by enslaved Africans, during which they forged a Christian tradition that responded more appropriately to their concerns and condition. Considered conspiratorial by planters, these meetings were illegal and could result in severe punishment.[2]

This was the beginning of the Black church as an invisible and illegal institution. It originally formed for two reasons. One was for slaves to have a more liberating worship experience and, through contextualized Christian formation, their own practical theology. The other reason, for slaves who weren't as radical in their worship practices, was that it provided an alternative to White churches in the South, where Blacks were not allowed to be part of the worshipping community. In many of these churches, Black slaves had to stand outside and listen to the worship service inside or glimpse it through an open window or door.

The White church in the Deep South before the Civil War provided the theological justification for the institution of slavery. During the Jim Crow segregation period following the war, White churches continued to provide the theological justification for segregation. And even in the North, where Blacks were allowed to worship in White churches, in many cases they had to worship in the back of the sanctuary or up in the balcony.

The Black church had to be underground and invisible because it was an illegal church whose core was the spiritual and physical liberation of Black slaves. The preaching, singing, and praying in the Black church were centered in scriptural texts such as the story of Exodus. The law of the land for Blacks was slavery, but the focus of the church was on a God of deliverance. This is why the original Black church was not in a building but outside in the woods. Sometimes slaves had to meet late at night so that no one would see or hear their songs and cries for freedom. It was truly an underground church.[3]

After the Civil War, the Black church moved from an underground church to a Black church within a so-called separate-but-equal society. This social context set the stage for the church as a whole in the United States to develop in a matrix of Black and White. Race has thus always been a significant factor in the church in the United States, regardless of revivals, baptisms, and denominational developments. Even today, the church is influenced by both the class and racial dynamics that surround it. It is from the reality of this context that the need for the post-Black, post-White church has grown. But even with the need for a post-Black, post-White church, the Black church has much to offer in the development of multi-ethnic and missional ministry.

The fact that the Black church survived slavery and Jim Crow segregation provides a unique opportunity to rethink the very foundation of what makes a healthy and strong church. Through all of the social challenges surrounding it, the Black church from its beginning has been about evangelism, worship, discipleship, global missions, community development, and leadership development. It played a major role in the development of historic Black colleges as well as civil rights organization such as the National Association for the Advancement of Colored People and the Urban League.

With such important contributions to the fabric of the United States, the Black church can continue to offer its many gifts to the post-Black, post-White church.

About the Gifts

When I refer to post-Black theology and ministry, I am not calling for the end of the Black church. Far from it. I am referring to the fact that a number of theologies in the Black church can be a gift and blessing not just to the Black church but to the broader body of Christ cross-culturally. It does not mean an end to Black theology. Post-Black ministry means that ministry practices coming out of the Black church can also be a blessing to the broader body of Christ. Historically, and to a large degree even today, the belief is that what goes on in the Black church is for Black people only. In most cases, non-Black people attending those churches understand this. They know that the ethos of the church is Black, and it's not their place to try to change that. They see themselves as being adopted into the ethos and family that is the Black church. My point here is that the development of multi-ethnic and missional churches would offer the gifts of Black theology and ministry to the broader body of Christ. We have seen this before in the United States, though it wasn't called "post-Black theology and ministry."

Black Power or Beloved Community?

The civil rights movement was a stunning example of post-Black theology and ministry. Dr. Martin Luther King Jr. led the movement for equality and justice that began within the Black church and community but soon became multiracial and multicultural. Black preaching was used to cast the vision of the beloved community, present the strategy of nonviolence, and provide the courage to face violent attacks. During marches in Chicago, Atlanta, Selma, and elsewhere, the songs of the Black church provided spiritual energy to proclaim and advance the core purposes of the movement. Over time the church services, rallies, and marches become multiracial, which is what makes them post-Black. The gifts of the Black church were shared with and received by a broader group of believers for social action and transformation.

Some leaders of the Black power movement didn't agree with Dr. King's post-Black approach. Theologian James Cone makes note of this when he defines and defends Black Power and connects it to a Black theology:

> There has been and still is much debate among the critics of the Black Power regarding the precise meaning of the words. The term Black Power was first used in the civil rights movement in the spring of 1966 by Stokely Carmichael to designate the only appropriate response to white racism. . . . What does it mean

when used by its advocates? It means complete emancipation of black people from white oppression by whatever means black people deem necessary. The methods may include selective buying, boycotting, marching, or even rebellion. Black Power means black freedom, black self-determination, wherein black people no longer view themselves as without human dignity but as men, human beings with the ability to carve out their own destiny. In short, as Stokely Carmichael would say, Black Power means T.C.B., Take Care of Business—black folk taking care of black folks' business, not on the terms of the oppressor, but on those of the oppressed.[4]

Black Power leaders believed that the movement should be Black only. They saw the empowerment of Blacks as something that was a higher priority than equality with Whites. Their goal was to escape from White oppression. This position is viewed by some as a move away from a Christian-based approach through the beloved community to a Black humanist approach. Carl Ellis takes this position when he writes about the crucial turning point in the civil rights movement that led to the rise of the Black Power movement:

> Midway through the Memphis-to-Jackson march (1966), many began to chant Black Power, Black Power! Stokely Carmichael, the new leader of the Student Non-violent Coordinating Committee (SNCC), openly challenged Dr. King to take a stand for Black Power. Shock waves spread across America. A consciousness change was taking place among Black leaders, signaling the beginning of the Black phase. With it, White humanism was dead and buried, and Black humanism was born.[5]

Black Power leaders believed that the agenda for the liberation and equality of African-Americans would be compromised by making the movement multiracial, so their sole focus was Black Power. In fact, they viewed pursuing friendship with White "opposers" as catering to Whites and not putting a strong enough focus on Black empowerment. They didn't understand the ultimate outcome of King's vision of the beloved community, which he laid out in a message, "The Challenge of a New Age," delivered in 1957. In it he said that what he referred to as "the end" was reconciliation and redemption. He saw a love that would transform opposers into friends, goodwill that would "transform the deep gloom of the old age into the exuberant gladness of the new age. It is this love which will bring about miracles in the hearts of men."[6] In using the phrase "the end," King was pointing to a new creation—something beyond Black and White. His pointed us to the new heaven and the new earth that God will create in the return of Christ, which is the end of all things and the beginning of things at the same time:

> And I saw a new heaven and a new earth; for the first heaven and the first earth passed away, and there is no longer any sea. And I saw the holy city, New Jerusalem, coming down out of heaven from God, made ready as a bride adorned for her husband. And I heard a loud voice from the throne, saying, Behold, the tabernacle of God is moving among men, and He shall dwell among them, and they shall be His people, and God Himself shall be among them, and He shall wipe every tear from their eyes; and there shall no longer be any death; there shall no longer be any mourning, or crying, or pain; the first things have passed away [Revelation 21:1–4].

This end vision for King was the kingdom of God. It was about the ending legal racial segregation, hate, and inequality. Finding identity in Black or White Power in and of itself is part of old humanity, sinful humanity. In King's beloved community, God's children would live in equality and harmony. The civil rights movement was post-Black because it began to embody what it was pursuing. As the movement became multiracial, it was manifesting King's vision of meeting a radical reality. It is a gift of the Black church that transcends its origins.

The civil rights movement provides a blueprint for the types of churches we need today, and King's preaching and his writings are the basis for post-Black theology. We need churches that are not only pursuing the vision of the kingdom of God but embodying the kingdom of God. If there is no racial segregation or homogeneity in the kingdom of God, why should there be in the church?

The civil rights movement was about the Black church developing and then inviting people of other races into post-Black ministry. It was a visible expression of the Christ-centered and multi-ethnic picture of the kingdom of God. It did a lot to transform society, but it didn't do much to transform the racial makeup of the church, which is why the need exists for post-Black theology and ministry today.

The Black church can once again play a significant and transforming role in society by taking the lead in the development of multi-ethnic and missional churches. African-Americans are not the fastest-growing ethnic group in America, but just as God did with the Jews, he can use a relatively small minority to advance his church. God delivered the Hebrew people from oppression in Egypt and made a covenant with them. Although they kept turning away from God through idolatry, which led to exile after exile, God kept pursuing them and using them to his glory. What if he desires to do this today through the African-American church? Could God delivering African-Americans from slavery and Jim Crow segregation be for a greater purpose? I do not believe that God authored this type of oppression for a greater good, but I believe that he can get glory on the other side of the sinful acts of humanity through an oppressor's own free will. The civil rights movement is evidence of this type of God's work.

Many other gifts within the Black church can be a blessing to the broader body of Christ, as preacher and Christian sociologist

Tony Campolo understands. In his well-known sermon "It's Friday, But Sunday's Coming," Campolo talks about the influence of the Black church on his life and gives it much honor and respect.[7] It's obvious in his preaching that the unique Black preaching style has deeply influenced him. He has received and used this gift to have a broader influence for the kingdom of God.

The post-Black church represents an opportunity to take a societal reality and use it to advance the kingdom of God, much as Black music has, for example. The blues, jazz, and the Motown sound began as Black music and over time became America's music and influenced an array of artists. Today, the same thing is happening with hip-hop. Hip-hop is more than music; it's a culture that influences music, language, fashion, and values. Through multi-ethnic rap groups such as the Black Eyed Peas, hip-hop is the music of the world, and it's shaping broader adolescent and young adult culture. As these art forms have moved beyond Black culture to become national and international, they have become post-Black.

What if the Black church had this kind of influence in terms of national and global kingdom advancement? This is not only possible, but it is a must. The post-Black church could be one solution to the American church in crisis, serving as a missional, kingdom-advancing church within an ever-increasing multi-ethnic and multicultural reality.

Gifts for the Multi-Ethnic and Missional Church

Although the gifts that I refer to within the Black church are not unique to the Black church alone, the emphasis here is on how the Black church contextualizes these areas. This contextualization can become a gift back to the larger church in engaging both a multicultural world as well as a world of injustice. I specifically look at how

the Black church has contextualized worship, theology, shepherding, and being missional. Certainly there are more issues that could
be looked at, but I believe these areas are important places to start.

Worship Gifts

The experience of worship within the Black church is truly a gift
that the multi-ethnic and missional church can use in many ways,
starting with Black preaching. Many people seem to believe that
only African-Americans can master this style of preaching, but some
of its key elements can be a gift to the broader church.

Black preaching in its truest form is rooted in the Word of God.
Gerald Joiner, currently senior pastor of Zion Missionary Baptist
Church in Louisville, Kentucky, begins all of his sermons by saying,
"There is a word . . ." From there he goes into the main scripture
text for his sermon. There is a distinct rhythm to how he leads the
congregation into the Word of God, which he learned from his
own pastor and passed on to me when I served as associate minister
with him at Redeemer Missionary Baptist church in Minneapolis.
Beginning the sermon this way points to both the authority and
centrality of the scripture, a device not unique to the Black preaching style. What is unique is how Black preaching begins with the
Word but then, through exegesis, points the community of believers to action for social change. European-American and evangelical
preaching tend to be focused on the individual, with individual
applications. Black preaching is directed more to the community
and its responsibility to change social conditions. This "sending"
element of the Black preaching style is what makes it a missional
gift to a church.[8]

These other aspects of Black preaching are also gifts to the
church:

- It is about preaching to a community, a specific community of
  people living in certain conditions in need of transformation.

- It begins with the Word of God and then reveals how the Word of God applied can be used by a community of people to bring about the justice and transformation of God.

- It begins historically as a word of personhood and liberation upon a slave people. Black preaching reveals the God of liberation and shows how applying this Word about God brings about freedom and justice.

- It ends with celebration that points to hope in Jesus's resurrection. By ending with celebration, the congregation is both inspired and empowered to go out into society as change agents. They are motivated as sent people to work for kingdom advancement and the forging of the beloved community in the world.

- It is participatory. This celebration at the end of a sermon is the call to go forth. This is why call-and-response is also a unique element of Black preaching. Black preaching at its best is not just about what the preacher is saying but about the exchange between the preacher and the congregation. This is the congregation saying in essence, "Pastor, we're with you." When the preacher says something the people feel, they respond, "Amen," "Say it, preacher," or "That's right." In this way, preaching is both a passionate and a participatory act. White pastors can demonstrate a passion for what is being preached about and invite the congregation to join this element of corporate worship.

My point here in describing the gifts of Black preaching is not to get White pastors to pressure their congregations into responding to preaching the way that Black congregations do. But what would happen if White preachers invited worshippers into the sermon? They could invite individuals from the congregation into the sermon based on giftedness. I've asked people in my congregation gifted at dance, poetry, or rap to respond to major parts of the sermon. I do this through a worship design team made up of people within the congregation who are gifted in the arts and bring various elements of the creative arts to supplement and strengthen the sermon. In this way, the sermon becomes bigger than the preacher and truly becomes a corporate act of worship.

Preaching is at the core of the experience of worship within the Black church, but there are other elements that can serve as gifts as well. The entire flow of the traditional Black church worship experience, in fact, can help create a missional ethos within the church.

At Redeemer Missionary Baptist Church in Minneapolis, where I grew up, worship began with the church's ten deacons and deaconesses standing before the congregation. After the initial hymn, they read scriptures as a devotion. Just like the sermon, the preservice devotional was rooted in the Word of God. It created an ethos that the Word of God must enter into the space for there to truly be an experience of worship.

The deacons and deaconesses all had southern roots, so the hymns they introduced and invited the whole congregation to join in had words that not only lifted up God but also pointed to a slave and segregation history. "Swing Low, Sweet Chariot," for example, combined biblical story, the anticipation of heaven, and a heritage of a people crying out to God for freedom. For a missional church to be a sending church, there must be a remembering of where a people have come from in order to gain a greater sense of where God desires to send us now. To be sent into a multiracial and multiethnic world for kingdom advancement, we must remember our racial and ethnic past.

After the singing, the deacons and deaconesses knelt and prayed. Their prayers ranged from those for members of the church who were sick and in the hospital, to issues of poverty, incarceration, and unemployment. They prayed against injustice in the physical realm and against an evil and demonic force that needed to be cast down in Jesus's name. The entire church over time would participate in these prayers, crying out in unison for healing, peace, reconciliation, justice, and empowerment. This was indeed a missional exercise.

Next, the choir processed in, and there was an official call to worship. The songs of the choir were communal and focused not just on what God desires to do in the life of an individual or family, but what he desires to do through a people who have historically known oppression and second-class citizenship. Right before the sermon, the pastor invited the congregation forward for altar prayer. This was a time of corporate prayer for the surrounding community, not just for the needs of those coming forward. Once again the congregation was praying in unison, crying out to God for his kingdom to come on earth as it is in heaven.

I believe that the unique worship experience of the Black church can be a blessed gift to the multi-ethnic and missional church. A preacher within the multi-ethnic and missional church should work to develop a connection with the congregation that calls for a response, even if that response is a smile or the decision to leave the worship experience as God's vehicle of justice in the world. There ought to be a general freedom of worshipful expression. In a ethnically diverse church, the goal should not be to get everyone to say, "Amen" or "Yes, Lord," but to create a freedom of worship where everyone can find a place in the faith community. Allowing people to use their creative gifts to participate in the experience of worship transforms the congregation from primarily an audience that watches the spiritual performances of a select few to a body worshipping in unison.

Theological Gifts

Theologies of justice, liberation, and reconciliation are also gifts that can be a blessing within the multi-ethnic and missional church. These theologies developed over time in the Black church in the midst of the injustice of racism and slavery. The Black church was founded as both a liberating community and a justice-focused institution.

It is liberating to the degree that it brought personhood and the invitation of salvation to Black slaves who had been stripped of their formal African and tribal identity. The church affirmed their identity in Christ.

The Black church is also historically an institution of justice to the degree that it played a role in the freeing of slaves. Black pastors served as freedom fighters in the early days of the Black church. Sermons and spirituals were about the message of salvation in scripture and contained code language for a strategy to be freed from slavery.

The organic theology of God identifying with the oppressed drives the core identity of the Black church, shaping the justice and liberation theology that is essential to this church. James Cone speaks to the importance and influence of the Black experience in Black liberation theology:

> What does it mean to speak the truth from a black theological perspective, that is, what are the sources and the content of theology? To explore this question we must begin by exploring the theological function of the black experience. There is no truth for and about black people that does not emerge out of the context of their experience. Truth in this sense is black truth, a truth disclosed in the history and culture of black people. This means that there can be no Black Theology, which does not take the black experience as a source for its starting point. Black Theology is a theology of and for black people, an examination of their stories, tales, and sayings.[9]

Although Cone's intent is the development of a theology for Black people, there is a gift here as well to the broader body of Christ in studying theology through the Black experience. Cone's theology speaks of a God who is mindful and identifies with those who are marginalized and oppressed. The church can be liberated and better positioned to reach a multicultural reality when it is willing to rethink theology from the perspective of historically marginalized and oppressed people.

Another gift is a biblically rooted strategy for loving your enemy and seeking reconciliation, which the Black church cultivated through the civil rights movement. At the core of the movement was nonviolence, which was fueled by the agape love shown to us by Jesus in the scriptures. King spoke to this transforming love: "Agape means understanding, redeeming good will for all men. It is an overflowing love which is purely spontaneous, unmotivated, groundless, and creative. It is not set in motion by any quality or function of its object. It is the love of God operation in the human heart."[10]

The love that is needed for equality and justice in the world is the same love of God shown in Christ Jesus that brings about new life. This is the theological gift to the church. While most of the church has been divided in general between the church of evangelism and the church of social justice, this has never been the case within the Black church. The Black church has been able to see a God of new life and of justice. It has seen the love of God working toward the realization of both through Jesus Christ and the indwelling of the Holy Spirit. And that combination is what makes the Black church one of the strongest examples of being missional. For any missional church conversation to be authentic, the history and contemporary activities of the Black church must be considered.

Shepherding Gifts

The shepherding gifts from the Black church are best seen in its pastoral mentoring and development. I've been mentored in unique ways over the years by African-American pastors who have played a significant part in how I live out my calling in a multi-ethnic and missional context. A major reason for this is that my calling into ministry was originally affirmed and developed within the Black church.

I wrestled with a strong sense of a call to ministry during my senior year in college. At the time I was attending Rising Star Missionary Baptist Church with my fiancée, Donecia. Her grandfather, Edward Berry, was the senior pastor. After church service one Sunday, I told him that I thought I was called to the ministry. He looked at me and said, "Really? Well, we'll find out about that." And then he simply walked away. I was confused by this response and, to be honest, somewhat disappointed. The next Sunday during the worship service, he shared with the congregation what I had told him the Sunday before: "Brother Efrem says he thinks he might be called to be a minister. Well, we're going to find out. In three weeks at 4:30 in the afternoon, Brother Efrem is going to preach his trial sermon, and after that we're going to vote on whether he is indeed called into ministry."

I couldn't believe what I was hearing! I thought that by approaching him, I was going to have a conversation and possibly some prayer around what I was wrestling with. Instead I had to prepare to preach a sermon in three weeks! That Sunday afternoon three weeks later, the small sanctuary was packed. Many of my family members were there too. After a couple of songs from the choir, Pastor Berry stood behind the pulpit and called me up to preach my first sermon, which I titled, "Give Credit Where Credit Is Due." I preached out of the Psalms on the importance of being grateful for all God has done for us. During the sermon, I felt the affirmation and support of the congregation as they spoke back to me: "Amen!" and "All right, young preacher!" When I looked back at Pastor Berry, he had a smile on his face, and I felt the love of that congregation.

After the sermon, I was excused from the sanctuary while the church went through a process that led to a vote. I was brought back into the sanctuary and told that the church had indeed voted to license me as a minister in training. Pastor Berry told the congregation that I was no longer Brother Efrem but Minister Smith. After many hugs and kisses from those in the congregation, there was a little reception of sorts for me. My entering into the ministerial call felt like a family event.

After this, I spent the next year and half being mentored and coached by Pastor Berry. On Saturday mornings, we met in his church office. We prayed together and went through the scriptures together, and he talked to me about what it means to be a pastor. In other words, he not only taught me; he modeled the role of pastor to me. I shadowed him wherever he went as a pastor. When he went to the hospital to visit church members, I was there. When he officiated a funeral, I was there. When he took communion to the homebound elderly, I was there. He would call me on the phone and quiz me on scripture texts or on topics within the systematic theology book that he gave me. I was in a traditional apprenticeship model of the Black church. I was learning, growing, and being pushed into a deeper understanding of what it means to be a pastor. I was in my own personal seminary experience, and I thank God for Pastor Berry.

After a year and a half, Pastor Berry said to me one Saturday morning, "You're ready now." He said he was putting a council together and that another associate minister in the church, Dennis Carter, and I would go before the council to be considered for ordination in the National Baptist Convention USA. He gave me two pages of questions to study based on everything that he had taught Dennis and me.

When I appeared before the ordination council, made up of ordained pastors and deacons from churches across Minneapolis and St. Paul, my anxiety was well beyond what I had felt that Sunday afternoon when I preached my first sermon. After I was grilled on a number of theological, church history, and ministry practice questions, I was excused to sit in a room with other young ministers there to be considered for ordination. Except for one person, we were all called back into the room with the ordination council and told that we would be granted ordination in the Minnesota State Convention of the National Baptist Convention USA. I was given the title of assistant pastor at Rising Star Missionary Baptist Church. I was ordained the following Sunday. This whole experience, from that initial sermon to ordination, was a spiritual rite of passage for me.

After Donecia and I married, we began attending the Black church of my childhood, Redeemer Missionary Baptist Church. The first Sunday that we attended, many families who had known me from the time I was a boy greeted me with hugs and smiles. Deaconess Mary Carson said, "You have to meet our new pastor," and took me to meet Pastor Gerald Joiner. The best way to explain my reaction when I first met him is to say that I'm 5'8 and he's 6'7. He stood up from behind his desk, walked toward me, bent down, and gave me a big hug. "I understand that you are a son of this church," he said. "Are you prepared to preach this morning?" A bit dumbfounded, I said I was.

I preached a sermon on the story of David and Goliath, a topic that came to me when he stood up and bent down to hug me. Donecia and I joined that church a few weeks later, and Pastor Joiner took over as my mentor where Pastor Berry left off. Over time, I recognized Pastor Joiner as my father in the ministry. I still call him Daddy Joiner to this day, and he continues to mentor me on what it means to be a fruitful leader in ministry.

Today, I'm fortunate to have a team of African-American leaders who mentor and coach me. I learned the importance of being teachable and have experienced fruitful ministry because of the shepherding I have received in the Black church. In addition to Pastor Gerald Joiner, I'm taught and mentored by African-American leaders within the Evangelical Covenant church such as Robert Owens, Stan Long, Brenda Salter-McNeil, Debbie Blue, Henry Greenidge, Harold Spooner, Jerome Nelson, and Don Davenport.

Regardless of your ethnicity, I highly encourage you to have wise African-American mentors in your life if your desire is to lead a multi-ethnic ministry. The multi-ethnic and missional church must receive the gift of shepherding development through apprenticeship and mentoring.

Missional Gifts

The missional gifts of the Black church can be seen in its historical and contemporary commitment to community development and engagement for kingdom transformation. This part of the missional Black church influenced my vision for planting the Sanctuary Covenant Church and the Sanctuary Community Development Corporation. The vision was planted within me in Evansville, Indiana.

I went to Evansville in 2002 when I was serving on the national training team for Youth Specialties, a company focused on building the capacity of local churches in the area of ministry to youth. While I was leading a one-day training session for paid and volunteer youth workers, an older African-American gentleman came up to me during one of the breaks. He asked me if I'd be willing to have dinner with him and then come and see his church. In truth, I wanted to go back to my hotel room after the training and watch March Madness college basketball, but I didn't tell him that. He was persistent, and I finally agreed.

After dinner, he drove me to his church, First Memorial Baptist Church. What I saw was amazing. The church owned a housing development that provided homes for seniors and low-income families. The church also owned a fast food restaurant that not only hired teens but also taught them entrepreneurial business skills. This Black church was having a significant missional impact on its surrounding community.

As I was flying home the next day, I thought about not only First Memorial Baptist Church but also the same kinds of things that had been done when I was growing up at Redeemer Missionary Baptist Church. When I was a child, Redeemer ran a co-op store and had a transitional housing program. When I served there as an assistant pastor under Pastor Joiner, we ran a computer learning center and partnered in the development of a shelter for abused women. As a pastor for youth, I wrote my first grant to the local neighborhood association and received resources to turn the lower level of the church into a youth activity center. These are just a few examples of the gift of community development and engagement that the Black church can give to the multi-ethnic and missional church. The missional work of Black churches in predominantly Black communities must be contextualized by multi-ethnic and missional churches.

In some cases, Black churches are in communities that are no longer mostly Black, and this has created a challenge. The community I grew up in Minneapolis was predominantly African-American for years, but the Asian, Hispanic, and Russian immigrant population has grown since then, and many of the historic Black churches in the area have struggled to reach out to the new diversity around them. Some purposely choose not to engage the diversity because they desire to remain a Black church. Robert M. Franklin also points out that many urban Black churches have become commuter churches, not community churches:

> The historical influence of the black churches appears to be in decline. Scholars have demonstrated that congregations in low-income communities have modest outreach to the surrounding community. Most black churches are commuter congregations in which a majority of members reside one or more miles from the sanctuary. Their members tend to lack profound knowledge of the local neighborhood and do not offer a broad range of social services to their neighbors.[11]

Franklin was mostly focusing on the Black church reaching surrounding communities that are predominantly African-American and low income in cities like Chicago, Detroit, and Atlanta. But in many cities today like Minneapolis, these churches are experiencing post-Black growth. If the Black church desires to be missional in many urban centers in America, it will have to become multi-ethnic. The best way forward is for these churches to train emerging African-American pastors with the ability to minister cross-culturally. This is a main part of my calling now in my role as a regional superintendent. I must do what Pastor Berry did for me with the younger generation of ministers: mentor and coach them and prepare them to lead in today's realities.

I take the apprenticeship model that equipped me for ministry in the Black church and apply it in a multi-ethnic context of my denomination, which is predominantly European-American. This kind of multi-ethnic and missional mentoring must continue in Black churches and denominations as well. As communities are becoming more and more multi-ethnic around the Black church, this church must raise up emerging African-American ministers who can lead in the new reality. Black churches should plant churches through these leaders who are post-Black. This way we don't lose the Black church ethos that is a great blessing to the body of Christ. As long as race is still an issue in our country, we will need strong Black churches to play a role in offering unique gifts to the multi-ethnic and missional church.

Conclusion

The Black church has a rich history of compassion, mercy, and justice ministry in all of its core ministry areas. The development of the post-Black, post-White Church is not calling for an end to the Black church. Where there are predominantly Black communities, there is a need for the Black church. Because the Black church's theologies and ministry practices have been marginalized, we still need the Black church so that we might have an opportunity to receive its many blessings for us. At the same time, the Black church must adopt a post-Black vision, establish a leadership development plan, and in some cases create ministry initiatives for the new multi-ethnic future. The Black church can play a significant role in raising post-Black leaders. I am an example and am proud to be a product of the Black church. I will forever be grateful.

6

creating a
post-white
church

When most people think of the Christian church in the
United States, their mental image is usually that it is
a White church, with its various denominations and
churches. Surveys and research concentrate on the White church, as
do models for church growth, church planting, and church leadership. Terms such as *megachurch*, *emerging church*, and *missional church* are
driven by concepts, debates, aspirations, and frustrations within
the White church. Most of the people lifted up as the examples of
church leadership are White and male. If I were to ask the average evangelical to name great historic Christian leaders, more than
likely Billy Graham would be mentioned before Martin Luther
King Jr. In some cases Martin Luther King Jr. wouldn't even be
brought up. If I were to ask about today's influential Christian leaders, the list would still be exclusively or dominated by White males,
such as Joel Osteen, Bill Hybels, John Piper, Andy Stanley, and Rick
Warren. Whenever I'm in a conversation about the voices and leaders of the missional church movement, for the most part only White

males are lifted up, such as Alan Hirsch, Reggie McNeal, Mike Breen, and Darrell Guder. The church planting movement is dominated by predominantly White organizations such as Vision360, the Association of Related Churches, and the Exponential Conference. Even in the area of multi-ethnic and urban ministry, White males such as John Piper, Tim Keller, and Mark DeYmaz are seen as major influencers.

It seems as if an idea or concept concerning the church is not legitimate unless it is led by a White male. Even images of Jesus and other biblical personages like Abraham, Moses, King David, Jesus, and Paul to this day are depicted as White or European when in reality they were more Middle Eastern or Jewish in appearance. The ancient theologian Augustine is also depicted as White, though he was born in northern Africa.

The great dilemma of the church today is that we are living in an increasingly multi-ethnic and multicultural reality, but you'd never know it from the dominant picture of the church in the United States. Certainly the White church is a major force and influence in identifying and training leaders and current thinking about new forms of church and innovative ways of thinking about and being church. I don't deny that reality. But it is not the complete reality by any means.

It's also true that many European-Americans and others in the White church don't see it as White. Like the staff member at the Sanctuary I mentioned in an earlier chapter, they consider themselves color-blind. They see the White church as neutral, even normal. Just as the mental image of the average American family is a White family of four living in a middle-class suburban neighborhood, the image of the average American church is a White church in a middle-class suburban neighborhood. European-Americans don't refer to their churches as White; they tend to describe their church instead by its denomination, theology, location, size, or leader. They also wouldn't necessarily recognize what kind of cultural influence and power their church has simply by being predominantly White, in the same way they might not realize the potency of White privilege.

The White church's influence and power is due in part to its history. One could argue that the decline of the church in the United States of America is more about the decline of the White church in the midst of a growing multicultural reality, in which European-Americans will eventually not be the majority in the United States. The reality of globalization is already moving the center of the church from the United States and Europe to Africa, Asia, and South America. This could mean that although Europe and the United States have led the missionary movement for the most part in contemporary history, these two places will eventually be the mission fields targeted by African and Asian missionaries.

To truly understand missions, we must go back to the scriptures and the missionary efforts of the first apostles. In the New Testament, the church at Philippi was the first Christian church planted by Paul on European soil, although it was not the first church he had planted: that was the church at Antioch, near Antakya, Turkey, which is close to Syria (Acts 13:1–3). This means that the first churches were not European or predominantly White. Neither will the churches of the future be White. It is interesting to me that the first churches and the future churches have something in common: both are multi-ethnic and are a picture of the kingdom of God.

The Challenge

The journey of the White church to a post-White church will not be an easy one. Many influential White megachurch pastors are not willing to lead into a new multi-ethnic and missional future regardless of the demographic realities. Neither are many White pastors of medium and small-size churches post-White. But it is the White megachurch pastors who have a significant influence on the broader church in the United States. When these pastors lift up a ministry idea or model as important, it seems to be taken seriously and adopted by many smaller churches. White megachurches have had the advantage of being resourced enough to step out in front of the rest of the church, pioneer new models, and create movements.

I believe that White megachurch pastors are unwilling to be strong advocates and proponents of the post-Black, post-White church for two reasons. One is that many megachurches are hidden from the reality of multicultural diversity. Some of these churches are located in less diverse rural towns where their weekly attendance outnumbers the town's population because Whites who live elsewhere, sometimes in more diverse communities, are willing to drive many miles to attend these churches. In many cases, the lead pastors of these churches live in communities that aren't very racially diverse either. So because of their isolation, many predominantly White churches have chosen not to become multi-ethnic and missional. Few Whites who attend those churches are even aware of the White ethos or the privilege they've developed within the church because of it.

The second reason could be because many of the White lead pastors do not have a strong background in multi-ethnic and missional issues. It's hard to put on a conference at your church on a topic that your church has yet to become fruitful in. Instead of admitting this, some pastors try instead to play down the importance of multi-ethnic and missional ministry. If White megachurches as a whole were to be fully honest about the pressing need for all churches to become multi-ethnic and missional, they would have to reinvent themselves on a number of levels, including the experience of worship, staff and leadership makeup, and theology. I include theology because it is at the core of this huge challenge. Theology would reveal that the multi-ethnic and missional church is biblical, which would naturally lead to the conclusion that a church with roots in a race-based society is unbiblical. This is the theological tension that causes so many not to want to deal the reality of the White church.

Another part of the challenge is that until the reinvention process of the White church took place, White megachurches would no longer be seen as the experts on the cutting edge. To a large degree, this is an issue of economics. A lot of money is swirling around large church conferences these days, and losing it would be a huge sacrifice for some.

But there is an answer. Megachurch conference leaders could admit the realities, note that that they have a lot to learn, and feature keynote speakers who point to future multi-ethnic and missional ministry models. Bill Hybels of Willow Creek Church and Ministry Association in Illinois is an example of how this can work. Willow Creek today is a true example of a White megachurch that has become multi-ethnic and missional. By Hybels's admission, the church still has a way to go in this area, but it has become a post-White church in terms of weekend attendance, and the experience of worship has become more and more multi-ethnic.

We have a long way to go in the development of post-White churches, but we should not be discouraged. The good news is that there are many examples already. I'm fortunate to be part of a post-White movement within the Evangelical Covenant church (ECC), and I will focus on it in this chapter. I use the ECC as an example not just because it's the denomination that I'm part of but also because it is one of the most diverse, predominantly White church movements in the North America. Close to 30 percent of the churches within the ECC are ethnic or multi-ethnic. The ECC is made up of eleven ministry regions known as conferences, each led by a superintendent. Of the eleven superintendents, three are African-American, one is Native Alaskan, and one is a European-American female. At the national level are ministry departments led by executive ministers. The executive minister who leads the Department of Compassion, Mercy, and Justice is an African-American female. This is just one glimpse of how the ECC has evolved over the years from a Swedish denomination to a predominantly White denomination made up of various European-American ethnic groups, to an ever-increasing multi-ethnic movement. This story is worth sharing as a blueprint for the development of multiple post-White churches and movements across the United States and beyond.

The Evangelical Covenant Church in Brief

Because the ECC is a relatively small denomination, it has developed into a multi-ethnic denomination without the notice of many denominational and church observers. With this being the case, as people discover the ECC, they might think that its efforts in the area of multi-ethnic ministry as well as initiatives of compassion, mercy, and justice are new. This is not the case. The ECC has been missional since its founding over 125 years ago, and its focus on being multi-ethnic goes back as far as the late 1960s. There may be some Covenanters who would make the case for work toward this end who go back even further. This does not mean that the ECC has become the perfect multi-ethnic and missional denomination by any means. But it does provide an example of a journey for predominantly White churches and denominations to consider as they work to become post-White. The ECC has never called attention to its work in multi-ethnic and missional ministry, but that doesn't diminish the significance of its impact.

　　To understand the ECC's approach and commitment to multi-ethnic, missional ministry, it's important to know a bit of its history. The brief sketch I provide will identify some important elements of how a White church can become multi-ethnic and missional.

An Immigrant Identity and Heritage

The ECC story is deeply connected to historic European immigration to America. As Kurt Peterson tells us, "Between 1850 and 1920, more than 1.2 million Swedes, approximately one-fourth of the population of Sweden at the time, immigrated to the United States as part of the deluge that brought more than 35 million Europeans to North America during the century of immigration from 1820 to 1924."[1] These Swedish immigrants were not so much gathering in the Unites States to form a denomination as much as to form community and forge missional lives:

> The Evangelical Covenant Church, organized in 1885, has its roots in the Lutheran Reformation of Sweden. The awakenings of the eighteenth century under the influence of the Halle Pietists and the Moravians coming from Germany, and the revivals that swept Sweden in the nineteenth century through the influences of Methodist George Scott and Lutheran Carl Olof Rosenius, who had been so much touched by the Moravian Herrnhuters, prepared the way for the birth of the Covenant. These stirrings of the Spirit were inevitably structured and organized. The conventicles—small gatherings of people for purposes of Bible study, prayer, and sharing—were led by lay preachers called colporteurs who began as booksellers and soon became powerful witnesses to the saving power of Christ. These conventicles were to be found in various parishes. In time the conventicles from several parishes were organized into mission societies. In time these were organized along district, regional, provincial, and eventually national lines.[2]

Both the immigrant and missional roots of the ECC are important. One of the ways for the White church to become post-White is to engage and embrace its ethnic and immigrant past. As I noted previously, ethnicity (but not race) is a biblical source of identity. The White church must move beyond being a racialized church to an ethnic and multi-ethnic church. One of the ways that normative Whiteness is sustained is through Whites acting as if they have no ethnic identity or past. It is as though only other ethnic groups have ethnic identity. This can happen in some cases because Whites want to be excluded from being part of an ethnic group if they take a color-blind approach to race and ethnicity.

The fact is that all Whites have an ethnic identity and heritage: Irish, British, Danish, German, and so on. It is important for Whites to engage their heritages to be able to find their rightful place within a post-White, multi-ethnic community. That is a biblical approach to dealing with ethnic diversity. When the White church is willing to engage the ethnic heritages that are represented among the Whites in their congregations, they will be able to live into the fact that they are already multi-ethnic. Then the new multi-ethnic and missional reality to be pursued is one that tears down the dividing wall of race.

The ECC is in a position to become a multi-ethnic movement not by denying its Swedish ethnic identity and heritage, but by embracing it. It becomes post-White by simultaneously embracing this identity and heritage and also pressing toward a kingdom and multi-ethnic future.

I would encourage any White church that desires to become post-White to begin not by focusing on reaching other ethnic groups but by assisting the congregation in uncovering their true multi-ethnic identities. As an African-American in the ECC, one of my fears is that the European-Americans in our denomination would lose a sense of their Swedish ethnic and immigrant heritage and find their identity in normative Whiteness. In some cases, this has already happened.

One of the reasons the drift from specific European identities into Whiteness took place among immigrants is that it was a road to prosperity within the United States. Whiteness became a way to move from being part of the working-class poor to the middle-class and even upper-class ranks of American life. As different White ethnic immigrant groups—Italians, Poles, Irish, and Jews—were marginalized or discriminated against because of their backgrounds, they found advantage in downplaying or even negating those identities. But becoming separated from their identities may have prevented them from developing a more authentic Christian community. Zenos E. Hawkinson wrote about the blessing of connecting to one's ethnic past in order to look to the future:

> Those of us who have worked at translating these Swedish songs of the Pietist heritage know that they are beautiful and tough-knit lyric celebrations of the personal discovery that even the wanderer on the road in the company of friends has the possibility of God's companionship. I am fully aware that I speak as a college teacher with a quarter-century of experience at the same place. Some wanderer! Middle-class, with the hope of Social Security coming to me along with a pension, I have spent most of my life teaching middle-class virtues to my kids, which includes not being uprooted, being where you ought to be when you ought to be, playing guitar in church but not on the open road. I can only read the accounts of immigrant kids—six years old, seven years old, ten years old, twelve years old—coming with tags around their necks to Castle Garden in New York.
>
> Meanwhile, I recall my twenty-one-year-old son, strong as a moose and healthy as an ox, wanting to go alone to the East

Coast, and my response: "Not until I got some proper idea of what you're gonna do there'" We have reached the point where we can laugh about that now (at least I have). The record of the immigrant experience shows how fragile a human life is, and yet how extraordinarily resilient it can be—how impossible it seemed that anything could survive that earthquake, and yet how remarkably the earthquake was survived, and with what beauty. New shoots sprang up in some of the least likely places in the world. After the storm there was a new growth. Those who lived through it, however, could hardly have appreciated those possibilities. And I am simply offering the observation that this is happening to us right now. In my bones I feel that we are being uprooted now in a variety of ways, personally and communally. We are pulled in strange directions, led out, as it were, by fishhooks and captors, in one direction or another, dispersed all over the world. Little wonder that people feel so small and vulnerable to attack, just as were our forebears, who nevertheless found strange places and moments of unutterable anguish and loneliness, suddenly a comforting hand and a voice says, "You are not alone. I have purposes. I have things to be done.". . . Our own tradition in the Covenant Church gives us reason to have confidence that people can be thrown bodily out of their accustomed culture and can create new things as a consequence.[3]

We see in Hawkinson's words a powerful connection between the history of an immigrant people and looking toward a new future in the midst of present tensions and realities. This is how to become a post-White church: look to a past beyond Whiteness in order to forge a post-White future. Getting beyond Whiteness through an engagement with an ethnic and immigrant heritage can create a bridge with other ethnic groups that already have a high value of their own heritage. When Whites engage their ethnic identities, they can better identify with the stories of other ethnic groups and their importance to their present journeys.

Black History Month is very meaningful for me as an African-American. I make a practice every February of reading books and watching documentaries that allow me to reengage my own ethnic heritage. When I was the pastor at the Sanctuary Covenant Church, I would preach on the connection between stories in the scriptures and those within the African-American experience. Some staff and some parishioners questioned why I would do this, and some European-Americans wondered why there even needed to be a month set aside to consider the history of African-Americans. Some African-Americans in our congregation were offended by this attitude and responded with something like this: "Whites have a cultural dominance throughout the whole year. Why can't we have a month that focuses on our history as a people?"

For the sake of building a reconciling community, I took a different approach. I would agree that we should question whether a month should be set aside for Black history. Why couldn't we deal with the history of African-Americans throughout the whole year? And why not also expand beyond the history of African-Americans and look at Asian-Americans, Hispanics, and Native Americans as well? And then I would ask, "Why not rediscover the ethnic history of Whites?"

Black History Month for us became an opportunity to have greater post-Black and post-White discussions. As a member of the ECC, I have been moved by the denomination's commitment to remember and uplift its immigrant identity and also desire to be a multi-ethnic movement. Its Web site (www.covchurch.org) lists video resources that connect what the ECC is about today with its historic connection to the missional pietism of Germany and its influence on the Swedish church.

In 2010, the ECC celebrated its 125th anniversary. At the annual meeting of the denomination, held in Saint Paul, Minnesota, an exhibit traced its immigrant and missional history. I was part of a panel discussion on how the heritage of the ECC can assist in fueling the future.

When the ECC launched a new strategic planning process, Organizing for Mission, president Gary Walter began his initial presentations by reminding us of the initial missional yearnings of the founding mothers and fathers. He then tied that topic to a multi-ethnic and missional future opportunity for the denomination.

Remembering is important in the forging of a new reality that can engage a multi-ethnic reality. This remembering must be connected to biblical stories where God calls the people of Israel to remember their heritage and how God worked among them as a God of deliverance, mercy, and justice. As God worked these elements out through the ethnic group of Hebrews, he called them to be people of compassion, mercy, and justice to immigrants, the poor, and the marginalized among them. By forgetting their heritage and true identity, they ran the risk of not knowing their true mission and purpose. Could it be that the false identities of race have caused the church over time to not realize a broader kingdom mission and purpose?

Domestic Missional Roots

Another significant part of the ECC's roots is its focus on being missional. At the beginning, it didn't see itself as a denomination as much as a missions society. Most, if not all, European-American denominations have brought their global missional roots into their ministry practice today, and most have institutionalized world missions on some level. Even many recent church plants, once they get to a place of being self-sustaining, get involved in global missions by connecting to the efforts of their denomination, connecting to an organization such as World Vision and Compassion International, or creating their own global missions entity.

Where some European-American denominations have fallen
short is in forgetting their domestic missional heritage and failing to
leverage it for a greater missional future. What I mean by this is that
by becoming White, predominantly European-American denominations and churches have distanced themselves from being able to
better identify with immigrant and marginalized people. When you
forget your own immigrant and marginalized history, the immigrant
and marginalized people of today become "those people" instead of
"our people." Whiteness when connected with being well resourced
creates a privilege that creates distance with those of a different race
and class. In many cases, Whites have a history of coming from an
immigrant people group that was looked down on because of its
language and economic status. There are some cases where even
physical features caused European immigrant groups to be discriminated against. I realize that this is not the history of all Whites.
There were always wealthy, educated, and socially connected groups,
and there were slave owners as well. But there are enough of the
immigrant and marginalized stories to paint a new picture of White
history that can be healthy for a multi-ethnic and missional future.

The ECC has continued to stay mindful of its domestic missional past. The First Covenant Church of Minneapolis is one of the
oldest churches within the denomination. In its early years, it ministered to the Swedish immigrant poor as well as other European
immigrants in downtown Minneapolis. It was also a place of significant evangelism centered around passionate and powerful preaching.
The fellowship room of First Covenant Minneapolis has many pictures of the working-class Swedes who made up the church in the
early days.

Today the church is both multi-ethnic and missional, and it is
reclaiming its heritage by forging a new future. The senior pastor,
Dan Collison, is European-American, but the experience of worship
features Robert Robinson, an African-American and internationally

known gospel artist who leads worship on a monthly basis. The church has a day care and preschool, Metro Kids, that ministers to families in downtown Minneapolis and other neighborhoods in South Minneapolis.

This church is living into the future without forgetting its immigrant past. The broader White church needs to do the same. It was the church historically that played a strong role in developing ministries of mercy in the United States as well as overseas. The church has played a role in starting hospitals, orphanages, and schools for the poor in this nation. Though there were some White churches that supported slavery and Jim Crow segregation, we cannot forget about the many White churches and denominations that stood for freedom for slaves and justice for the marginalized. The White church must recover its missional roots by rediscovering its past involvement in ministries of mercy and justice here at home.

Some churches and denominations have deep historical roots in both mercy and justice, and others more in mercy. Ministries of mercy can also be described as ministries of charity, for example, a food pantry or a clothing ministry. Ministries of mercy are very much needed today. Ministries of justice are more about the empowerment of people. They begin by getting at the root causes of why families in a surrounding community need food, clothing, and other necessities. Understanding the root causes of the challenges of a surrounding community will bring up both issues of individual responsibility and systemic issues of injustice. Responding to the issues of systemic injustice is what leads to the development of justice ministries. Justice ministries usually take on two approaches: advocacy and direct services intended to empower the recipient of the services. Advocacy might include dealing with slum landlords, underfunded schools, or a lack of viable businesses for economic viability in a community. Direct service could include tutoring, job training, or housing programs. The ECC has used its historical commitment to ministries of mercy to move to a more holistic approach of developing ministries of compassion, mercy, and justice.

The Missional Ministry of the EEC's Pacific Southwest Conference

The history of my own conference, the Pacific Southwest Conference, may be a useful example of the principles I'm discussing here. The conference was informally organized in 1902 as Kingsburg Colony Covenant Church, six churches in California that came together to form the Svenska Evangeliska Missions Foreningen. It was officially chartered on May 24, 1906, and would later be called the Swedish Evangelical Missionary Association of California. Eventually, through a strong commitment to church planting, it came to be known as the Pacific Southwest Conference.

Church planting led the movement to domestic missional opportunities beyond California and the development of a multi-ethnic mosaic that went beyond the original Swedish identity. By 1927, the conference, now with eighteen churches, had established a retirement home, a nurses' home, a sailors' home, and a hospital. Within various conferences throughout the early history of the ECC, additional retirement homes, nurses' homes, and hospitals were developed.

Although the Covenant church was small at its beginning and had limited resources, being made up of farmers and blue-collar workers, it was able to minister to the local poor and needy. Over time these ministries of mercy led to the development of the Covenant Ministries of Benevolence, which led to Covenant retirement communities, hospitals, and initiatives for at-risk and vulnerable children. These roots point to immigrant churches that had a transforming impact on society through ministries of mercy.

Local Covenant churches and Covenant laypeople have been part of other domestic missional efforts that are nondenominational.

One of these missional ministries, Hospitality House Youth Directions (HHYD), was developed in Minneapolis in 1943 as Hospitality House Christian Center by the Christian Businessmen's Committee of Minneapolis (CBMC) to minister to servicemen on leave during World War II.

After the war, it became a child placement agency until the late 1950s.[4] By 1960, the CBMC had a new director, Elwood "Woody" Larson, a Swedish-American man who was a graduate of Minnehaha Academy, a school owned by the Northwest Conference of the ECC and a member of a Covenant church in the Minneapolis area. He had a vision for Hospitality House to become a Christian boys' club to reach at-risk young men in North Minneapolis. At the time, North Minneapolis was changing from a predominantly Jewish community to one made up of mostly poor Whites and poor Blacks; it eventually became a predominantly Black community.

Larson officially started Hospitality House Boys club in 1961 with eighty-five urban boys meeting at an elementary and junior high school in North Minneapolis. In 1963 it became its own non-profit organization separate from the CBMC. By 1971, a girls' club was developed, and the name changed to Hospitality House Boys and Girls club. In the 1980s it had locations in both North and South Minneapolis. The South Minneapolis club was walking distance from my house when I was a child. A young African-American man named Keith Johnson was the Southside program director, and he and other staff drove through our neighborhood to pick up kids like me for athletic, educational, and spiritual growth programs. This was the first parachurch ministry that I would come to know as a child, and it was started by the missional efforts of a Covenant layperson.

My first ministry job as a adult was as the Southside program coordinator for Hospitality House Boys and Girls Club in 1993. I learned a lot about a holistic approach to Christian youth development through my work there. My boss was a man named Jon Kramka, who was a member of Community Covenant Church in North Minneapolis. Community Covenant had come to embrace the changing demographics over the years and had intentionally become a multi-ethnic church. Although North Minneapolis was an ethnically diverse community by the 1990s, its ethos was that of a Black community. Community Covenant Church was a church before its time: it had truly become a post-White church in a community where race could become a tense issue at any moment.

Not only was Community Covenant multi-ethnic, but through a partnership with Hospitality House Boys and Girls Clubs, it was missional as well. There was no competition in North Minneapolis between these two ministries on any level. They worked together toward transforming lives and community. Members of Community Covenant served as coaches within the athletic programs of Hospitality House, and as youth at Hospitality House came to know them, some of them began attending Sunday school at Community Covenant. This model of missional cooperation and partnership between churches and parachurches is still very effective today.

As I worked on staff with Hospitality House, I was moved by this humble and kingdom-minded partnership between Hospitality House and the church. When the Sanctuary Covenant Church was planted, we also developed a partnership with Hospitality House, now known as Hospitality House Youth Directions, and I served on the board for a couple of years. It was also important for us, as a Covenant church in North Minneapolis, to build a healthy relationship with Community Covenant Church as a multi-ethnic and missional church that had been serving the community for many years before our arrival. One of its members was a facilitator of the first Invitation to Racial Righteousness initiative that took place in 2005 at the Sanctuary. This was very important in our early days of developing into a church with a high priority on reconciliation. I was also able to develop a significant connection with its new senior pastor, Luke Swanson, who has continued to lead this church on the journey of being a post-White church. I realize now that both the ministries of Hospitality House and Community Covenant are part of a significant missional heritage of a post-White movement within the ECC.

Engaging the Model for the Future

Remembering a missional heritage provides missional identity for today and into the future, and it must be engaged and implemented in new ways within the context of a multicultural reality. One of the ways to do this is by connecting the theology and principles for ministries of mercy with a theology and principles for ministries of justice. The ECC's rich missional roots of ministries of mercy, like many White denominations, go back to the late 1800s. But it is another matter for White denominations and churches to bring justice into their missional practice. Nevertheless, it remains a biblical mandate and is crucial to the development of a post-White church.

Providing the Space to Deal with Race and Justice

The civil rights movement of the 1950s and 1960s created the atmosphere necessary for White denominations and churches to begin to deal with issues of race and justice in new ways. Two things were at work at this time. First, White flight was taking place in urban communities as Whites moved to the suburbs and African-American, Hispanic, and Asian families began to move into cities. White churches that had existed in these communities for years had to decide whether to integrate. If they moved out of these communities, what would become of their church buildings? A second dynamic was the assassination of Dr. Martin Luther King Jr. in 1968, which led to riots in cities across the United States. This was also a significant time in the post-White journey of the ECC.

In 1969 what was know as the Missions Board of the ECC was separated into two independent departments: the Department of World Mission and the Department of Home Mission, which eventually became the Department of Church Growth and Evangelism.

I begin this story with Reverend Jim Sundholm, who was serving at the time as the senior pastor of Community Covenant Church in North Minneapolis. A number of tense yet needed conversations were taking place in the ECC during the 1960s and 1970s around the issue of race and urban ministry, and he was part of those conversations, as were a number of African-Americans. It was actually the courageous and fiery voices of African-American pastors, such as Bill Watts and Willie Jemison, that prophetically called the ECC to a missional journey that would include justice. These and other African-American leaders were pressing the ECC about its commitment to the urban community and to African-Americans in particular.

Another important person was Robert Larson, who at the time served as director of urban church planning. He brought into the ECC not only new strategies for urban church planting but also for the beginnings of ethnic-specific church planting. The ethnic-specific or homogeneous unit principle model for church planting helped lead the ECC into a new post-White reality. I realize that today, the homogeneous unit principle as a model for church planting can be criticized by proponents of the multi-ethnic and missional church, and I am one of those critics, but for a White denomination to begin the journey of being post-White in the 1960s and 1970s, this was a needed approach. Even today, there are White churches that begin the journey of being post-White by starting ethnic-specific and homogeneous churches within their existing White church.

Under Larson's leadership during the 1970s, a conference was held every year with a focus on urban ministry. This conference became the place for the needed conversations on urban ministry and justice to take place and would, at a grassroots level, influence how the ECC would live out being missional domestically. Out of these conversations came the Urban Commission; next, a focus on ethnic ministry was added to form the Urban and Ethnic Commission of the Evangelical Covenant Church. In the beginning, this was mainly a Black and White conversation and initiative, but it planted the seeds of a multi-ethnic movement.

What is important to learn from this portion of the ECC story is that for the White church to become post-White, it must make space for authentic conversations about race and justice to take place. It's not enough just to pursue ethnic diversity within the White church. In order to be both multi-ethnic and missional, conversations about race justice must take place.

Some White churches don't make progress in becoming post-White; although they want ethnic diversity, they don't want to deal with the White ethos that is already deeply rooted in the church and hard to challenge. I've been involved in White ministries that said they wanted diversity but didn't want to be challenged around issues of race and justice. Sometimes White churches use theology to avoid these issues by trying to present social justice as unbiblical. Other times they may try to avoid the issues by saying that race is not an issue at their church and it's the African-American, Native American, or Hispanic individual who has the problem. The person of color gets painted as too sensitive, angry, or unable to work with White people. Churches that create this kind of environment for people of color are fighting against being post-White. They are actually fighting against becoming the beloved community that in their hearts they desire to be. The ECC was willing to provide the space through an urban conference to have the necessary uncomfortable conversations to become post-White.

Intentional Ethnic and Multi-Ethnic Church Planting

While tense meetings around urban ministry were taking place in the 1960s and 1970s, Robert Larson was working with other ethnic leaders to plant and adopt new churches. Initially the department that he would eventually lead focused on ethnic-specific churches made up of Eskimos, Hispanics, African-Americans, and Korean-Americans. The Central Conference of the ECC was where most of the initial multi-ethnic development took place, which made sense because Chicago was the location of the national office. In California there were emergent African-American, Hispanic, and Korean churches as well.

These ethnic-specific church plants were important in the post-White beginnings of the ECC, and African-Americans continued to be the strongest voices pushing the ECC on issues of justice and race.

Another major turning point came through Henry Greenidge, an African-American minister who approached Robert Larson with the idea of planting a multi-ethnic church within the ECC in Portland, Oregon. Larson was somewhat reluctant about this model, but Greenidge went on to plant the first multi-ethnic church within the ECC in 1988. Irvington Covenant Church in Portland still exists today as an example of a post-Black and post-White church.

As more African-American, Asian-American, and Hispanic pastors came into the ECC, ethnic-specific ministers associations were created. Henry Greenidge and Pastor Don Davenport were two of the first heads of the African-American Ministers Association of the ECC. These ethnic-specific minister associations would lead to the separation of the Urban and Ethnic Commission. Today the ECC has an Urban Commission and an Ethnic Commission made of the heads of the various ministers' associations representing African-Americans, Asian-Americans, and Hispanics.

Intentional Decisions and Relational Pathways

Greenidge's work to pioneer the first multi-ethnic and missional church plant of the ECC happened at a time when church planting in general would play a role in the significant growth of the ECC. It would also be how the ECC would grow into being authentically post-White by eventually having close to 30 percent of its churches being ethnic and multi-ethnic.

Gary Walter, now president of the ECC, was an important leader in this church planting movement. Walter served as a pastor of a Covenant church in Southern California, became director of church planting for the ECC, and then became the executive minister of the Department of Church Growth and Evangelism. He would say that both intentional decisions and relational pathways led to the ECC's becoming post-White. Intentional decisions came about through leaders such as Robert Larson, Paul Larsen, and other senior leaders who were willing to make the necessary hard and uncomfortable decisions about organizational restructuring, reexamination of core values and ministry priorities, and willingness to sacrifice personal views that weren't biblical.

The ECC's intentional decisions helped to restructure a denominational institution so that it could become multi-ethnic and missional. It has done this in two ways. First, the development of the Department of Compassion, Mercy, and Justice a few years ago moved justice issues from conversations within an urban and ethnic conference to initiatives to help local churches respond to challenges in their communities. This department is led by Debbie Blue, the first African-American woman to become an executive minister within the denomination. She provides leadership to initiatives to move the ECC forward in multi-ethnic and missional ministry. Both the Sankofa Journey and the Invitation to Racial Righteousness develop awareness and capacities around cross-cultural issues for church leaders. The department has held think tanks on issues such as immigration and incarceration and played a key role in the development of a biblically centered resource paper on compassion, mercy, and justice. This department drives and works to sustain a domestic missional ethos throughout the ECC as post-White churches move past ministry initiatives of simple charity to community development models centered in biblical justice.

The ECC's other intentional decision was to set a measurable goal of crossing the 30 percent threshold of ethnic and multi-ethnic churches within its latest strategic plan. Connected to this is a continued commitment of multi-ethnic representation throughout the denomination staffing structure. An assessment tool, the Five-Fold Test, was created to assess the progress made in this area.[5] The tool, created by Gary Walter and Harold Spooner, president of Covenant Initiatives of Care, identifies five areas to consider for authentic multi-ethnic and missional development:

1. *Population.* This asks, "Is there an increase in the numbers of people of different ethnicities represented based on real population growth?"
2. *Participation.* It's not enough to just look around and have a diversity of faces. The question becomes, "Are people engaging in the fellowship, services, meetings, and events of a church or denomination?"
3. *Power.* The question within this area is, "Are the positions and structures of influence such as boards, committees, and executive staff positions being held and influenced by the perspectives and gifts of diverse populations?"
4. *Pace setting.* With the diversity now experienced, the question is, "What new ministry opportunities is the church or denomination now better positioned to strengthen and initiate?"
5. *Purposeful narrative.* Over time the multi-ethnic diversity experienced on all levels of a ministry should lead to the development

of what will become a new heritage for future generations. This also leads to a church or denomination moving from just multiple ethnic-specific stories to a unified story through the realization of the beloved community. The question to wrestle with in this area is, "How do all of these multi-ethnic and diverse streams flow together into one story moving forward?"

The way in which I came into the Covenant was truly a relational pathway that can only be attributed to a work of God. In 2002, I was on the staff of a United Methodist church in South Minneapolis. That summer, a multi-ethnic and missional church in Jackson, Mississippi, asked me to become their next senior pastor. I felt a call to the office of senior pastor in Mississippi, but my heart was still very much in Minneapolis. I felt that God still had something for me to do in the city where I grew up.

A couple of weeks after making the decision not to stay in the process with the church in Jackson, I was having lunch with a couple of friends. As I was getting ready to leave, I saw Jon Kramka, my boss when I worked at Hospitality House, sitting in a booth. He was now working for the Northwest Conference of the ECC, and we scheduled a time to meet for lunch a couple of weeks later.

I shared with him over lunch that day about feeling called to be a senior pastor but not feeling called to go to Jackson, Mississippi. He then asked me if I had ever thought of planting a church. I hadn't and told him so. He then told me that the director and associate director of church planting for the ECC would be in town the next week and wondered if I would be interested in meeting them. A week later, I was meeting with the director of conference ministries, Jon Kramka, associate superintendent for the Northwest Conference; Mark Stromberg, director of church planting; Dave Olson, an associate director of church planting; and Don

Davenport. I shared with them for the first time a vision for the church of my dreams.

A few months later, my wife, Donecia, and I went through the Church Planters' Assessment Center of the ECC. The next year, the Sanctuary Covenant Church was planted. This is an example of a relational pathway. If the White church wants to become post-White, ask God to leverage relationships that you already have across race to his glory.

Relational pathways have led to the Covenant's post-White reality in amazing ways. The Covenant's connection with parachurch organizations such as InterVarsity has led to many leaders of color coming into the ECC as church planters of multi-ethnic churches. An Asian-American church planter named Peter Cha was working to plant a second-generation Asian-American church, Parkwood Community, in the suburbs of Chicago with the help of an Evangelical Presbyterian church. This church was hoping that Cha and his group would join their denomination, but there were other relational pathways at work in the early life of this church plant. As Greg Yee tells it,

> Parkwood's pastoral team leader Peter Cha sought the counsel of his former homiletics professor at Trinity Evangelical Divinity School, David Larsen, brother of then Covenant President Paul Larsen. This time of discernment ultimately led a group of Parkwood's pastors and lay leaders to a Midwinter Conference and conversations with Central Conference leaders Herb Freedholm and Craig Anderson, executive director of the ministry Don Njaa, and director of church planting Gary Walter. Parkwood experienced a growing sense of chemistry and convergence with the Covenant, especially as the denomination pushed into the third year of its church planting focus. Covenant leaders exhibited an intentionality that would

eventually help pave the way for Parkwood to be adopted as the Covenant's first second-generation Asian American church at the 1997 Annual Meeting in Anaheim, California.[6]

Parkwood was a multi-ethnic church because the initial core team was made up of Chinese, Japanese, and Koreans. Peter Cha's relationships with other Asian-American second-generation leaders such as Greg Yee and Dave Gibbons led to other multi-ethnic, second-generation and Asian-American-led churches coming into the ECC across the United States.

This again shows how important relationships and key conversations are to the development of post-White movements. Relationships can work to lead White churches into a post-White future. Relationships can also assist the White church in creating a post-White church movement through the planting of ethnic-specific and multi-ethnic churches.

Conclusion

Most of the time when I talk to European-American pastors and other congregational leaders about the need to become multi-ethnic and missional, they don't respond defensively. If there is any discouragement, it is mainly in wondering how to move forward in this ministry venture. I tell them that I believe Whites begin by rediscovering their ethnic and immigrant past. This gives them an opportunity to connect their identity with the ethnic heritage of the chosen people of God, the Israelites. By remembering their history and through Christ, this group becomes a truly multicultural and kingdom people. This story can be incorporated into the White church so that it can become a post-White church.

The post-White church must also be willing to have what can be tense conversations about race and justice. Though uncomfortable, these conversations are needed in the development of the multi-ethnic and missional church. If they are grounded in prayer and there is a willingness to listen without defensiveness, they can be fruitful.

One place for the White church to start on the journey to becoming post-White is by developing partner ethnic-specific ministries within the existing congregation. This ministry cannot just be a ministry initiative where good White people are doing something good for Asians or Hispanics, for example. It must be an opportunity for the White church to grow, learn new ways of being church, and even have their existing ethos dismantled. The White church can also be part of planting intentionally multi-ethnic and missional churches. Consider relationships that you already have or that can be built with churches of a different ethnic makeup. There may be members within the existing White congregation who are just waiting to be empowered to be a part of a core team made up of people different from them to forge a new post-Black and post-White church.

Finally, those in the White church must consider intentional decisions that will eventually reinvent their church as they currently know it. There are structural changes that need to take place in order for a White church to become post-White. A church must be willing to look at its board, committees, and staff structure in order to make room for a diversity of faces, gifts, and perspectives.

We are at a critical time in the life of the church in the United States. The White church can join a movement that will lead to the development of multi-ethnic, missional, and beloved communities.

7

leadership

I n 2003, when I embarked on a journey of planting the Sanctuary, a church that I hoped would be intentionally evangelical, multi-ethnic, missional, and urban, I felt I was totally prepared. As I've already recounted, since the day I became a Christian as a teenager, I'd had a passion that the church should be a community that breaks down the walls of racial division and deals head-on with injustices. The mentoring I received from Bart Campolo and Art Erickson increased my commitment to ministry that was multicultural and urban with a high priority on the holistic development of youth and community engagement.

The Black church had influenced my passion to plant a church focused on kingdom justice, and the multi-ethnic Park Avenue United Methodist Church influenced planting one committed to reconciliation and community engagement. After college, I had worked full time in urban youth ministry at Hospitality House Youth Directions, a parachurch in North Minneapolis, and had been a youth minister at Rising Star Missionary Baptist Church, also in North Minneapolis, as well as serving at Park Avenue United Methodist Church as an associate pastor overseeing youth ministry and community outreach. I volunteered as a youth minister within another African-American church, Redeemer Missionary Baptist Church in South Minneapolis. I served as a youth pastor at a predominantly European-American megachurch just outside Dayton, Ohio. I had a seminary degree from Luther Seminary in Saint Paul. And right before the founding of the Sanctuary, my wife, Donecia, and I had recently been through an exhaustive assessment for church planters within the Evangelical Covenant church and had been approved. That's a lot of experience. I didn't see how I could be better prepared.

But with all of this experience, passion, and preparation, four years into the planting of and leading the Sanctuary Covenant Church, I was planning my exit strategy. This was not because the church wasn't doing well. We had grown to be a church of close to one thousand people in attendance, with about four hundred members and strong ethnic diversity. On top of this, we had also started the Sanctuary Community Development Corporation, which focused on youth development, job readiness, and community engagement.

With all that, I was still ready to quit. I was burned out, holding grudges against other people in the church, upset with other pastors in the community, and constantly in need of affirmation. The church was doing well, but I was not. What was wrong with me? I had gone through the church planters' assessment center and seemed to pass with flying colors. I was the senior pastor of a growing church. I was being invited to speak at conferences, and within the first three years of the church, I'd written two books. But yet I didn't feel very successful. I wasn't sure what was wrong, but I was clear on areas in my life and ministry where I was feeling stressed and not happy with myself.

During this same time, I had gone to Atlanta to attend a gathering of African-American church planters from my denomination and sat through a session led by a pastor from Boston who had been serving in a church for over twenty-five years. He shared with us wisdom for serving as a pastor for the long haul. One statement that he made I'll never forget: "Never get too hurt, too angry, too lonely, or too tired in ministry." He used an acronym for this: HALT. Basically he was saying if you were struggling in these areas as a church planter or pastor of a church that has years of history, you needed to halt and consider your own spiritual health. Notice something else that he is saying though. By using the word *too*, he was recognizing that pastors indeed get hurt, angry, lonely, and tired, and to deny this reality is unhealthy. Dealing with these feelings is a part of being in ministry, even for Jesus, as we can see in the gospels. He was hurt physically. He was angry when he confronted those turning the temple into a marketplace that took advantage of the poor. He was lonely on the cross and feeling isolated and abandoned by his Father in heaven. He was tired as he said those final words on the cross: "It is finished."

These feelings are part of the experience of ministry, but the issue to be careful of is when, as a ministry leader, you find yourself in a sustained state of hurt, anger, loneliness, or tiredness. This is where I was. I realized then I needed to halt in some way, but I didn't know how. I just knew that I was struggling with all those feelings. Specifically, I was struggling with preaching, congregational relations, interactions with other pastors in my local community, and balancing family with increasing numbers of outside speaking engagements. I had failed to address how these areas were affecting me. More important, I lacked a plan of spiritual and leadership development. In all of my ministry experience, I had never had someone coach me on these two important issues: spiritual health and leadership development. These critical issues pointed to something beyond my direct and diverse ministry experience. There are both natural and supernatural challenges when it comes to leading the post-Black and post-White church.

The Need for Spiritual Health and Leadership Development

Anyone with a desire and passion to lead a multi-ethnic and missional church must recognize the importance of spiritual health and leadership development for all ministry leaders, particularly for those leading post-Black and post-White churches. The reason for attention to spiritual health is that spiritual warfare comes with the development of multi-ethnic and missional churches.

I dealt earlier in this book with the structure of race as being a part of the fall of humanity and racism being a sin. I would go even further and describe racism as a demonic force that contributes to God's creation's not living in unity the way God desires. Race and racism are not dismantled through reconciliation between human beings alone. They must also be dealt with as evil and spiritual strongholds. Satan is waiting to attack those who threaten these strongholds. The post-Black and post-White church as a force of the kingdom of God takes on not just the evil force of racism. It also takes on all those other strongholds of bondage and injustice in the surrounding community and beyond: addiction, gang activity, poverty, unemployment, and broken families. If these were purely natural issues that could be solved by the power of human beings alone, then why haven't they been dealt with already?

Those who lack a spiritual warfare theology, or what is known as a theodicy (a theology of evil), will struggle with this and may not see spiritual health as a priority. This was the case with me. Growing up in the mainline church for the most part, I didn't really have a theology of spiritual warfare. I did believe in Satan, but I didn't necessarily see Satan as being at war against me because of my passion to follow Christ by growing as a disciple and planting a church that would resemble his heavenly kingdom. Spiritual health is about recognizing the warfare factor as well as the continuing journey of growing as the beloved child of God. The ability of a pastor to be emotionally healthy is directly connected to his or her willingness to make spiritual health a priority.

The reason leadership development is important is that leading a multi-ethnic and missional church does not come naturally for many people, but it is crucial for all of us living in this race-based society. We must develop ourselves as leaders from a cross-cultural and multi-ethnic perspective. We may think that because we live in a diverse community, this isn't something that we need to address in our lives. Or we may take a "color-blind" approach to dealing with ethnic and racial diversity. Being able to lead a multi-ethnic and missional church calls for the ability to navigate the challenges and complexities of our multicultural and multiracial world.

Another reason for leadership development is that there are still relatively few multi-ethnic and missional churches, and so that puts pressure on leaders. When this kind of church grows and has a fruitful impact, the leader quickly becomes an expert. This was my story. Because the Sanctuary Covenant Church grew the way that it did, soon I was seen as a national expert on multi-ethnic and missional churches. I wasn't totally ready for this. I had not learned how to prioritize my life in a healthy way when all the speaking engagements came. I also wasn't prepared for the natural threat that the post-Black and post-White church is to the existing Black church and White church.

I began to understand the importance of developing a leadership development plan after meeting with a spiritual director and taking a class, "Overcoming the Dark Side of Leadership," my first year in the doctor of ministry program at Bethel Seminary. Through both of these experiences, I was able to zero in on the areas where I was struggling and the places where I needed health and development. I began to see myself not only from the perspective of the spiritual warfare within multi-ethnic and missional ministry but also how I was influenced in my behavior by issues not dealt with from childhood and other ministry experiences that hadn't been reconciled. I had not fully confronted experiences of being teased for the color of my skin or because of my broad nose when I was a child. Prior to planting the Sanctuary Covenant Church, I had worked on staff for predominantly European-American churches and parachurches. There were experiences that, at least to me, were connected to race and ethnicity, were not resolved, and needed healing. The combination of all this was coming out in how I interacted with leaders of the various ministry areas of the church and through behaviors that were at the core of my struggles. Because of unresolved issues connected at least in part to my to race, there were moments when I was easily offended by Whites but would work hard to not express what I thought because I felt that I needed to keep up my reputation as a chief reconciler.

The Struggles I Face

It might be useful to other leaders who are involved in post-Black and post-White churches to take each of the leadership issues I faced—preaching, congregational relations, interactions with other pastors in my local community, and balancing family with increasing numbers of outside speaking engagements—and consider the insights I have gained about them. These may not be all the issues facing multi-ethnic and missional leaders, but they provide a framework for laying out a context for why this kind of ministry can be challenging and cause burnout if they are not addressed.

As you read through the areas of challenge for me, consider the issues and areas that challenge you the most. Each of us faces unique issues and areas that cause struggles for us based on our own gifts, strengths, weaknesses, and experiences around race, ethnicity, and diversity.

Preaching

Although people within my congregation would be surprised to hear that I was struggling with preaching, I realized more and more that this was a problem area for me, but not for the reasons you might think. Preaching is one of my spiritual gifts, so that wasn't the problem. Rather, the problem was my constant need for affirmation. It seemed that after every sermon, I needed people to affirm that the sermon was good and had importance to their lives. I found myself looking for people to tell me that the sermon was not just good but great. I would fool myself by saying that I was merely looking for feedback, both good and bad, but really what I wanted and what I felt I needed was affirmation.

Every week, I would ask our worship leader, the associate pastors, one of the elders, my wife, and random members of the congregation what they thought of my sermon. If they told me that it was great, I felt good inside and was able to go home and enjoy the rest of the day. I used the affirmation of my sermons as fuel to prepare for the next one. It was as if the affirmation of the sermon was tied to a broader affirmation of me as a person and as the senior pastor of the church.

And when someone said that the sermon was just okay or he or she had problems with my preaching, I took it very hard. I'm not saying that I don't still struggle with this, but at the time, I was in denial about what was at the core of this struggle. One example of this struggle was an Easter sermon I preached where I talked about the need to be connected to the authentic biblical Jesus versus one who divides us by race by lifting up a White Jesus or a Black Jesus. Using John 15 as my biblical text on the title, "Abiding in the Vine," with the vine being Jesus, I raised the question, "Which vine are you connected to?" I talked about a church in the United States that seems to be clinging to multiple versions of Jesus. Some are abiding in the Black Jesus and others in the White Jesus. The big idea of the sermon was that if we are truly going to be a reconciling church, we would have to abide in the biblical Jesus, a multi-ethnic and multi-cultural Jesus who is both the Son of God and the Son of man. With passion, sweat, and tears, I preached about the biblical Jesus who is also relevant in an ever-increasing multi-ethnic and multicultural society. I also talked about racism as a demonic force and that force being behind to some degree the creation of the White Jesus.

The next morning, a man in our congregation, a European-American, called the office and expressed his anger with my sermon and wanted to know what the elder board was going to do about it. He complained that he was tired of these political and racial talks and wanted sermons preached from the Word of God. Even though we talked by phone and in person days later, I carried this around in my heart for a long time. Not only was I bothered because he didn't approve of a sermon that was focused on issues I'm passionate about, but because he happens to be a European-American male, I realized I was also was struggling with race issues that I hadn't fully dealt with. The issue here isn't about whether he (or I) was right or wrong, but more about my ongoing need for affirmation and about how I let this situation affect me and my ability to lead a post-Black and post-White church.

So as much as I love to preach and am gifted in this area, my need for affirmation created these moments of also feeling hurt, angry, lonely, and tired. One Sunday after preaching a sermon, I was so overwhelmed with this struggle that I fell into a chair backstage (we worshipped at the time in a high school auditorium), put my head into my hands, and began to cry. Our worship leader, a couple of the elders, and my wife tried to comfort me while asking me what was wrong. I remember just saying over and over again, "I don't know if I can do this anymore." This episode led to the elders' asking me if I needed to delegate more ministry responsibility to other staff members so that I wouldn't feel so weighted down. I appreciated their concern, but that wasn't the core issue. It was about my emotional and spiritual health.

It was also about the realization that my emotional and spiritual health is directly tied to my intimacy with God and my identity in Christ. Those who are leading a post-Black and post-White church will be beset with emotional and spiritual stress. Where you get life and identity from can increase this stress. Instead of getting life and identity from God, I was finding life and identity from being a preacher. This was going on for two reasons. One was that because I'm gifted at preaching and enjoy it, I was getting life and identity in it. The other issue was that I wasn't spending the time I needed in prayer, meditation, and Bible study. I was praying and reading the Bible often, but most of the time, I was praying for the church and those within it and reading the Bible for sermon ideas and preparation.

I needed to spend time alone with God to be reminded of my true identity. By knowing that I'm the beloved child of God and living into this, I didn't have to depend on affirmation of my preaching to get through the week. But not addressing this issue of finding life, identity, and affirmation in God through Christ was showing up in other areas for me as well.

Staff Relations

At the Sanctuary Covenant Church, we were fortunate to have an ethnically diverse staff. When I left to become a regional superintendent, we had nine full-time staff: four European-American, four African-American, and one biracial. For a church that was started with the goal of being intentionally multicultural, this type of diversity should be celebrated. Certainly I was excited about this staff, but at the same time there were some tough moments, especially across racial lines.

At one point, there was tension between myself and a European-American staff member who oversaw communication, design, and media for the church. I'm a very extroverted person, and he is somewhat introverted and quiet. I sometimes assumed that he felt a particular way that later I found out was not the case. If I shared a devotional in staff meeting and he didn't say anything, I assumed he either wasn't interested in or didn't support what I was saying. The fact that he was White could have been feeding my assumptions at a level deeper than I would want to admit.

Eventually we had a major blowup in my office, which was a huge surprise to me. Now that I look back on it, the issue seems pretty silly. We were arguing over my request to put an insert in the Sunday morning bulletin. He felt the insert didn't carry the quality of the normal communication pieces in the bulletin, which he designed. I really didn't care about all that at the time because I felt the information on the inserts was relevant to the needs of some people in our congregation. Also, I wanted him to do it simply because I told him to. Although we worked to resolve our conflict and have been cordial with each other since, I remember and still carry around some unresolved issues with him in my heart. Many days I questioned if he respected me as the senior pastor of the church. Was my questioning on some level connected to my being African-American and him being European-American? Was it also connected to my need for affirmation? These were areas I had to be willing to explore if I was going to be a healthy leader of church that had multi-ethnicity and reconciliation as a major part of its vision and purpose.

On many occasions during this difficult time, I said to myself that I was going to meet with him and deal with this issue head-on. But when I would finally find time to meet with him, our conversation revolved on the weekly ministry report. We continued to meet weekly, but without diving into the hard work of moving beyond a simply diverse staff to a truly reconciling staff. I even let that situation cause me to question if other staff truly respected me as a leader and saw me as their pastor.

Interacting with Other African-American Pastors
in the Community

Soon after I became senior pastor at the Sanctuary Covenant Church, I began to struggle with feeling affirmed by some of the other African-American pastors in the Twin Cities. When I accepted the call to plant a church in North Minneapolis, I had a phone conversation with an African-American pastor who was already serving a congregation in that area. I had known him for a long time, so his affirmation of what I was doing was important to me. He asked me, "Why don't you stay in South Minneapolis where you've been serving at that Methodist church?" I had also taken some criticism from other African-American pastors for using elements of hip-hop culture in our corporate experiences of worship.

I remember feeling excited about a story in the *Minneapolis Star Tribune* newspaper on our church being multicultural as well as being cutting edge by putting on monthly hip-hop worship services. The Saturday morning after the story ran in the paper, I attended a city-wide prayer service made up of mostly African-American pastors. I was asked to preach a small sermon on the importance of prayer. Prior to my preaching, there was a concert of prayer where various pastors prayed on different topics. One of them prayed for revival in the city and for the truth of God's Word to come back into the churches of the Twin Cities and for "the things of Satan to be removed from the church." He specifically mentioned a church that had been in the newspaper for bringing hip-hop in the service and began to pray against this sort of thing. I sat there realizing that he was praying against me and felt utterly rejected as other pastors intoned, "Amen."

Because I grew up in the Twin Cities, a number of African-American pastors have known me since I was a child. When I became a senior pastor, I realized that my overall need for affirmation included theirs, in part because so many of my paid staff positions in ministry have been within predominantly White evangelical churches and parachurches.

I realize now that the need for affirmation from African-American pastors was in part to relieve any feelings of being perceived as a sellout for serving within the multi-ethnic but still predominantly European-American Evangelical Covenant church. The tension that I wrestle with is that I simultaneously am passionate about the church being a multicultural and reconciling community, but also want to be received well and have strong connections within the African-American church community. The issue for me might be more than just affirmation; it may be validation from African-American pastors that my pursuit of a multicultural church that engages hip-hop culture is not something that causes me to be an outcast from the African-American church community. I ask myself, *Why this is so important to me?* I have received affirmation from some African-American pastors and ministry leaders and am offered many opportunities to preach in their congregations. But I tend to focus more on those whom I perceived did not affirm and validate my calling to multicultural ministry.

Balancing Family and Other Commitments

The fourth area that I felt had contributed to burnout was the tensions that sometimes arise in balancing my opportunities to speak nationally and making my family a priority. I deeply love my wife, Donecia, and my two daughters, Jaeda and Mireya. I also have developed over time a passion to preach and speak beyond my opportunities at a local church where I served or within the Evangelical Covenant church denomination.

I believe that the opportunity to speak nationally and at times internationally is part of my ministry calling, but I've had struggles with balance and making decisions that show that my family takes priority. There have been times when I would use calling, the perceived need for additional income, and the need to get away from the daily grind of the local church to network with other ministry leaders to justify my absences. I've come to realize that my need for affirmation and my struggle with feeling hurt, angry, lonely, and tired have contributed to the cloudiness of my motivations for taking speaking engagements.

This cloudiness affects my relationship with my family. It stings my heart when my daughters say, "Are you going out of town again?" It also was tough when my wife said, "There are times when you go out of town and I'm angry and lonely until you return." I also had to be willing to admit that I enjoyed the affirmation I tended to receive when I spoke out of town, as well as the opportunity to see changed lives. When you're preaching in the same place on a regular basis, there is more opportunity for criticism. When you simply show up at a conference or as a guest speaker at another church, more than likely the response will be positive. One reason is that you can give a sermon that you've preached before and preach it better. There may be a number of factors at work, but the issue of affirmation is big one for me. I have to be careful not to let that need for affirmation become harmful to my family, which is my first ministry.

What I Learned

What I learned in struggling through these issues over time was not only that I needed to spend time with God for true life, identity, and affirmation but that I also needed authentic community with other people where I could share what I was going through. This eventually led to meeting consistently with a spiritual director, leaning on the support of close friends, and getting involved with a prayer and study group. I needed to let Donecia walk with me in these issues. And then I gave my wife, spiritual director, and close friends permission to tell me how they thought I was making decisions about speaking.

In developing healthier relationships with staff and other ministry leaders, I began to spend time with people outside a formal ministry setting. By golfing, bowling, or having coffee with people,

I was able to see a side of them that I didn't when we were in a strictly ministry environment. In these informal settings, I was able to let my guard down and interact with a person in a way that can bring about reconciliation.

Facing the Problem

Healthy leadership is crucial if the multi-ethnic and missional church is going to be healthy. It begins with understanding that this kind of ministry is hard but very needed. We cannot afford to romanticize multi-ethnic and missional ministry.

Both natural and supernatural challenges await us if we venture into this calling. Another way of looking at it is that there are both external and internal challenges. Multi-ethnic and missional ministry leads us toward external challenges within our society and internal challenges within ourselves that we may have never dealt with before. Preparing for these challenges is important. We have to be willing to be transparent about our own struggles as leaders to make a part of our journey ongoing spiritual and leadership development in areas that we'd rather not deal with. If we don't do this, the external challenges of ministry will bring them out of us in unhealthy ways. This was my experience. You may not have the same issues as I have, but I'm sharing mine so that you may be able to unpack your own.

I came to realize that the common theme in the four areas where I was struggling was the need for affirmation. But that realization was not enough. I needed to identify what was at the core of this need for affirmation that was affecting my preaching, staff relations, connection with other African-American pastors, and balancing family and national speaking.

I have already noted that I took a doctor of ministry course, "Overcoming the Dark Side," during the summer of 2009. At the end of the course, I felt liberated for the first time to acknowledge this need for affirmation and how unhealthy it was. This class was based on a book of the same name by Gary McIntosh and Sam Rima (who taught the course).[1] Through this class and the way in which I spent time with God while taking it, I was able to get to the core of why, after only five years as senior pastor of the Sanctuary Covenant Church, I was feeling hurt, angry, lonely, and tired. The core that I'm referring to is the dark side itself. In the rest of this chapter, I will be referring to my dark side traits, which are narcissism and compulsive.

Some people refer to the dark side as the shadow side of a person. Whatever term is used, it's dealing with something in ourselves that normally we would want hidden; we might even deny that we have a particular trait. But under pressure and stress, this side moves from a hidden place to one where it is clear enough that others can see. The discovery of my dark side traits has allowed me to understand what is at the core of my need for affirmation from people. It allowed me to look at both beliefs and behaviors that may get in the way of the leader I wanted to be. I used the doctoral course to go through a process of looking at myself in a more holistic way and become a healthy multi-ethnic and missional leader.

This holistic approach is about contrasting our dark side with our light side, that is, our identity in Christ and the gifts God gave to us, which shape our unique kingdom purpose. But because at the time I was leading a multi-ethnic church that desires to be a reconciling community, I didn't want to do this work in isolation, so I approached the staff with the idea that they would join me on this journey. I think not approaching your spiritual health and leadership development on your own is a good strategy for pastors of post-Black, post-White churches. A holistic and team approach provides the benefit is that a multi-ethnic and missional church can become a reconciling community. Remember that the vision at the Sanctuary Covenant Church is to be "a reconciling movement." This tagline of sorts points to the original and larger vision statement of being "an evangelical, multicultural, holistic, reconciling, and urban community." The Sanctuary vision was another reason I didn't want to do this work alone. I was hoping there would be a benefit within a reconciling community of being transparent and presenting not only my faults before the rest of the staff but my desire to be healthy and live as a beloved being before them. This would mean not only taking a holistic approach of looking at my self but also devising a plan for development and growth.

To live as God's beloved takes the work of abiding in God's love daily. In order to live as the beloved, I knew I needed a beloved life and leadership development plan. The beloved life was about my spiritual health and beloved leadership about how I lead, manage, and serve others. Beloved leadership ought to come out of the overflow of the beloved life. I desired to do this work in community in order to grow more deeply in a reconciling relationship with them.

...ROHP
Date: August 27, 2014 at 12:39 PM
To: George Duey gaduey@aol.com
...t@mac.com

Sent from my iPhone

Begin forwarded message:

From: annette nabagala <annabaq2000@yahoo.com>
Date: August 27, 2014 at 10:24:16 AM PDT
To: Betty Duey <bettybyte1@mac.com>
Subject: Re: ROHP

Dear Mum

how are you,George,Donna,Brad,Glennis ,Kristine ,All the girls and boys ?
Thank you so much for my gift . I did find the money on my account , it was a surprise for me and i Have bought a nice cloth for the day at $155 and its taken to the tailor for tailoring and i have used part of the money to order for the cake of about 150 and am also going to use around $200 to buy a used computer for our ROHP office. i have decided to share the gift you gave me with Tezita and Winie. i will pay for winie's school fees and her requirements for school. winie's mum died of AIDS last year when she was senior Three and she was left helpless we now stay with her in our new house . Now she is Senior four. Tezita was scraped off the teachers payroll last month . thank you for the gift because it has made a difference to many of us and ROHP at large.
Nabagala

On Thu, 8/21/14, Betty Duey <bettybyte1@mac.com> wrote:

Subject: Re: ROHP
To: "Nabagala Annet" <annabaq2000@yahoo.com>
Date: Thursday, August 21, 2014, 5:37 PM

Thank you. I did the
wire transfer yesterday in the amount of $750. USD. Will
your bank charge you a fee?

The money is a "just because I love you
gift". Please use it as the Lord directs you, where ever
it is most needed. I pray that you will find just the
right dress for your wedding.

I love
you.

Betty

8

the beloved life and leadership project

The work of starting or leading an existing multi-ethnic and missional can be challenging. I learned over time that I needed to take ownership of my spiritual health and my ongoing leadership development. Part of this ownership was to put together a development project for our staff at the Sanctuary Covenant Church. We needed to take a holistic approach that would lead to a more reconciled leadership team rooted in intimacy and identity with God in Christ. This was the overarching theme for what would be called the Beloved Life and Leadership Project.

The Beloved Life and Leadership Project focuses on four areas: a personal profile, a servant profile, an intercultural inventory, and dark side traits. This project provides a holistic approach to the development of a multi-ethnic leadership team. In my case, by looking at myself holistically along these four dimensions and contrasting them with my four problem areas (preaching, staff relations, interactions with other African-American pastors, and balancing family and speaking), I could develop both my spiritual health and my leadership, both of them necessary in leading a multi-ethnic and missional church. I realize that spiritual health and leadership development are needed for servant leadership in any ministry context, but the focus here is on the term *holistic*. The biblical foundation for this holistic approach is found in Thessalonians and Colossians:

> Rejoice always; pray without ceasing; in everything give thanks; for this is God's will for you in Christ Jesus. Do not quench the Spirit; do not despise prophetic utterances. But examine everything carefully; hold fast to that which is good; abstain from every form of evil. Now, may the God of peace Himself sanctify you entirely; and may your spirit and soul and body be preserved complete, without blame at the coming of our Lord Jesus Christ. Faithful is He who calls you, and He also will bring it to pass [1 Thessalonians 5:16–24].

•   •   •

> If then you have been raised up with Christ, keep seeking the things above, where Christ is, seated at the right hand of God. Set your mind on the things above, not on the things that are on earth. For you have died and your life is hidden with Christ in God. When Christ, who is our life, is revealed, then you also will be revealed with Him in glory [Colossians 3:1–4].

To look at myself holistically, that is, in spirit, soul, and body, I began by using assessment tools that revealed more deeply my personality, spiritual gifts, intercultural competencies, and dark side. The ones I share are meant to give some ideas and provide a framework for this holistic approach. What's important for each person is to find the necessary tool to discover himself or herself more deeply in community. We also found it fruitful to bring in outside people to administer and assess the tools for us so that we understood ourselves better not only individually but also corporately. The tools and the outside perspectives become an audit of how we are doing as leader and staff in creating and leading a multi-ethnic and missional church.

This work is also connected to the importance of ultimately finding identity and life in Christ. Understanding ourselves more deeply, as well as reflecting on identity in Christ, will lead to a spiritual health and leadership development plan.

Going through this initiative in community with other staff allowed me to learn more about those I serve with and gave me insight for interacting better with them. We had to become the reconciling community that we were trying to create and lead. Some of what came out of this process I have brought with me and incorporated with the Pacific Southwest Conference staff I work with now.

This initiative took place over eight months at the Sanctuary. Every staff member took the various assessment tools and then participated in an all-staff development day in which we interpreted the results from a broad and collective standpoint. We also had individual coaching sessions with the project facilitators.

I've included in this chapter the rationale behind each assessment tool as well as a reflection of my particular assessment. Some of my reflections are also based on the journaling that I did throughout the process, time spent with my spiritual director, Tom Paige of the Center for Biblical Transformation, and a day alone with God that I took every month during the process. The initiative concluded with the development of both corporate and individual beloved life and leadership development plans, which were then integrated into a new strategic plan so that we might be a healthier and more missional church.

Digging Deeper into My Personality:
Insights Discovery Profile

One of the reasons I experienced burnout as a leader was that I didn't truly understand a deeper understanding the type of leader I am, and my need for affirmation was leading me to try to lead outside my natural abilities and gifts. In 2006, I had decided, again out of this need for affirmation, to prove that I was a real leader. I had been known for my preaching gifts for a while, but I was determined to show that I could also lead. And I could, but the way in which I was trying to prove it to others wasn't very healthy.

The leader profile I had adopted was based on the pastor as chief executive officer (CEO), which I had heard about and seen in action at many conferences. If the pastor wasn't a CEO or chief operating officer, then he or she was something like a visionary and motivational entrepreneur or president. In either case, the pastor was seen as a business leader with some sort of pastoral shepherding mixed in.

This is not to say that business principles and a business approach to leadership are bad. Rather, I began to see the church planter and senior pastor primarily through the lens of the business leader. This was directly connected to my desire to see the Sanctuary Covenant Church grow and my need for affirmation. Sam Rima speaks about this temptation to lead like a business leader.

> For too many of us who are spiritual leaders, ministry can quickly be reduced to just another career or profession at which we can be successful and make a name for ourselves. For those with entrepreneurial leanings the temptation is strong to treat church planting as something akin to a business start-up . . . acquire the financing, develop a business plan, create a compelling marketing campaign, and voilà—a successful start-up![1]

In many ways, this was my approach to the planting of the Sanctuary Covenant Church. I had put my business plan together, presented it to a number of suburban churches for funding, and saw significant growth within the first year. Then I wanted to see more attendance growth and other signs of success, such as budget growth. I began to study the leaders of successful churches. I would look at the list of fastest-growing churches and the list of the most innovative churches presented each year in *Outreach Magazine*. We were fortunate to make the innovative church list in 2007, but I had my heart set on making that fastest-growing list too. So I began to study the senior pastors of some of those churches. The majority of them were European-American, they were all males, and they all seemed to be visionary and entrepreneurial business leaders. I immediately felt somewhat inadequate because this was not my background.

I'm a visionary, but I did not feel like much of a business leader and have had no training to be one. I adopted the belief that being a preacher and theologian with an arts background was not enough. If we were going to be a successful church, I, as the senior pastor, was going to have to prove that I could be a real leader, like the ones in business.

We didn't have the resources at the time to hire an executive pastor, so I was going to be the executive pastor and the senior pastor. Acting as an executive pastor, I would need to be involved in staff development, finances, and building issues, but these weren't the areas of my strongest gifts. We also had created the Sanctuary Community Development Corporation, and I envisioned being the president of that as well. I was already the board chair, but this wasn't enough for me; I also had to be the president. I thought that by being all of this, I would be seen as a true leader and not just a preacher.

I had been very much in need for weekly affirmation as a preacher; now I was going to begin to need it as an executive leader as well. But by trying to become this executive and senior leader, I was not focusing on the servant and team approach that is vital to the development of a truly multi-ethnic and reconciling community. It can be argued that this approach is important in all ministry contexts, but when the church is about dismantling walls of division and creating multicultural community, it is nonnegotiable.

The holistic approach to staff development began with exploring my true and natural leadership gifts. I asked myself, *How am I really wired by God naturally (both strengths and weaknesses as well as growth areas and dark side)? Why am I not leading this way?* The dysfunctional and unbiblical approach to leadership that I had developed was not only connected to burnout but was also the way in which I was treating staff. Trying to lead in this way was directly related to the tension and blowup I had had with the communications staffer that I have already referred to. I was living in something that wasn't really me, and I was afraid to admit that because I thought that would be admitting that I wasn't a real leader. It wasn't that I couldn't supervise staff or lead beyond preaching on Sunday morning. It was more that I was trying to lead in a way that wasn't truly me. I was living in false leadership and a false identity.

In addition, I was making the church primarily about me when the church first and foremost is always about God. It is also about God's mission in the world of advancing his kingdom. The church is not ultimately about the affirming and the uplifting of Efrem Smith. Could it be that in some cases, pastors are competing with God for attention?

So it was important to discover not only what kind of leader I am but also the leadership and natural abilities of those I serve with. For this part of the project, we used the Insights Discovery Personal Profile assessment tool:

> The Insights System is built around the model of personality first identified by the Swiss psychologist Carl Gustav Jung. . . . Using Jung's typology, the Insights Discovery profile offers a

framework for self-understanding and development. Research suggests that a good understanding of self, both strengths and weaknesses, enables individuals to develop effective strategies for interaction and can help them to better respond to the demands of their environment.[2]

I learned through my Insights Discovery Personal Profile that as a leader, I'm a motivating inspirer, my learning style is one of interactive participation, and God made me a creative and visionary person. With a learning style of interactive participation, I'm at my best when I'm an involved team player. To be sitting in my office alone, trying to become both a senior and executive pastor, is not living in the reality of how God has made me. This rigid and dysfunctional business approach was feeding into my dark side and keeping me from the freedom of the beloved life: experiencing the liberation of living in my identity in Christ and in how God created me to function. Jeremiah comes to mind when I reflect on this: "Before I formed you in the womb I knew you, And before you were born I consecrated you" (Jeremiah 1:5).

Another one of my strengths is that I'm highly resourceful around people. My key strengths from the Insights profile showed that working in team and in community is exactly where I need to be. This approach is also important for a multi-ethnic and missional church. Part of the health of a multi-ethnic and missional church over the long haul comes from building strong multi-ethnic leadership teams. Some believe that the development of a diverse staff team is the hard part. This might be challenging for some churches, but it's not the hardest part or what leads to a healthy ministry. You can have diversity, but if the diversity is rooted in assimilation to the dominant group of people within the church, you're not achieving a truly reconciling and missional community. The harder work for the post-Black and post-White church is building a diverse leadership team that shares power and influence and ultimately leads to stronger outcomes for the church. My strong relational skills could be used in this work to empower people around me and thereby unleash their gifts and abilities. Those around me needed to feel that both their gifts and voice matter. What I was trying to be was the exact opposite of what is really needed in leading a multi-ethnic church. I needed to pursue who God has created me to be as the leader of the Sanctuary Covenant Church.

The Insights Discovery Profile also provides possible weaknesses that point to my dark side. Two in particular that I must acknowledge and manage are a tendency to exaggerate and the potential to come across as patronizing or superior. This makes sense knowing that my primary dark side trait is narcissism and my secondary trait is compulsive. My narcissism was coming out through using my gift of communication to make issues that were important to me bigger than they really were so that I could move an agenda forward. The exaggeration came in because some of the things I was making a big issue about weren't truly vital. As an example, let's say I wanted to bring a guest preacher in, and others in leadership didn't think it was a good idea or the right time. My narcissism would come out by communicating the blessings our church would miss out on by not having this particular speaker. But what if the opinions of others on this staff about not bringing that person in to preach were right? Would I be willing to not be so rooted in my agenda in order to get more insight on why they were pushing back?

My compulsiveness had to do with being overly concerned with how I look, which comes out in a couple of ways. One is that I care a lot about my appearance. My wife teases me because I sometimes iron my T-shirt when I am getting ready to go on a run or work out at the gym. (I can't believe I just confessed that!) I also care about how I look when I want to come across as the good guy in front of people. So there are times, not purposely I hope, that I would end up making someone else look like the bad guy so that

I could be the good guy. In the role play of good cop, bad cop, I want to play the good cop every time.

When I began thinking about the development of this project, I knew that I had to address how the dark side of leadership and the leader has an impact on leading a multi-ethnic church. If leaders do not manage their dark side, they can actually work against a Christ-centered, multi-ethnic, and reconciling community. In my case, knowing my dark side trait of narcissism, I realized that the church planter can easily become the center of attention. This has the possibility of spinning out of control if the planter doesn't acknowledge it and manage it through the beloved life. I'm proposing a servant-oriented and reconciling leadership that flows out of identity in and intimacy with Christ.

From what I discovered about myself from the Insights profile, my primary role as a leader is to cast vision and motivate others. It was important for me to understand that this is the role of leadership that God had given me to fill at the Sanctuary Covenant Church and even now as a regional superintendent. I must embrace this over a more executive and business model. By creating a beloved life and leadership plan, I move from being success driven to pursuing spiritual health and fruitfulness. My Insights profile as a motivating inspirer moves me from a self-focus to a focus on others and their becoming whom God has created them to be. As I find my identity in Christ rather than in myself, I become the beloved self. In the area of preaching, I no longer am focused on preaching for affirmation but being led by God to preach a word from scripture that motivates the hearers to be the people God has created them to be. It's also living in the biblical truth that ultimately God is preaching through me; it is not me alone preaching. My affirmation must come from God by living in the identity of the beloved self.

The inspirer in me is also a gift given by God to cast vision. This vision casting, which is part of my leadership call, should be

Spirit led and focused on the kingdom of God, not me. By using the natural gifts God has given me, I can fulfill my leadership call. Finding ultimate affirmation as God's beloved allows me to preach with more freedom. A scriptural foundation for this is Peter quoting the book of Joel in Acts: "But this is what was spoken of through the prophet Joel: 'And it shall be in the last days,' God says, 'that I will pour forth of My Spirit upon all mankind; and your Sons and Daughters shall prophesy and your young men shall see visions'" (Acts 2:16–17).

By understanding the gifts and abilities of the others on staff, I experience the blessing of our diverse leadership styles that God is using to develop a healthy and missional church community.

Understanding the Dark Side

The part of the beloved life and leadership initiative that focused on my dark side traits of narcissism and compulsiveness led me to reflect on the class I took in 2009. In one class, we focused on a personal narrative that gave me some insight into how my dark side of narcissism developed. It was important to look back on my upbringing and the role it played in the development of my dark side.

To this day, I remember vividly my first and probably most embarrassing moment as a child. It was third grade, and I had to go to the bathroom. I'm not sure why I waited so long to let my teacher know I had to go, but eventually I got up from my desk to ask for a pass to the bathroom. There were already two other classmates at the teacher's desk getting help on the classroom assignment for the day. By the time I finally was able to ask for the pass, it was too late: I was standing at the teacher's desk in front of the whole class with wet pants.

I was sent to the nurse's office to get cleaned up as best I could and put on some other clothes. I later went outside for recess wearing someone else's clothes. Worse, the word had gotten around school about my accident. That the majority of people who witnessed my accident were European-American, as was the teacher, also has not left me. I believe that being the center of attention in a negative way led to my narcissism.

As I grew up, I yearned to be the center of attention in a positive way. Instead of being teased or laughed at, I wanted to make others laugh and be the life of the party. Even as an adult, being in front of people and inspiring, entertaining, or making them laugh was life giving to me. I'm not saying that inspiring, entertaining, and making people laugh is necessarily bad. The issue is about health and where you're getting identity from. The ability to inspire people should be driven by a missional objective for transformation, not to replace something that happened in childhood.

As a child, I was very skinny, and though I loved sports and dreamed of being a professional football player, I wasn't a good athlete and participated in sports only until eighth grade. This particularly bothered me because it seemed that all of the other African-American kids were good athletes and I was the oddball. In addition, a lot of the images I saw on television of strong African-Americans were of athletes. In high school, I went to informational meetings for football and track, but would never try out for teams.

I eventually got involved in theater and music. I was very good at both and have natural ability. So while many of my African-American friends were going to football or basketball practice, I was auditioning for the school play. My sophomore year in high school, I sang a duet with a girl named Lavonne in the school talent show, and the audience gave us a rousing response. Every since, I've received affirmation when I'm on stage, which plays into my preaching. I sometimes find myself preaching and yearning for the same affirmation and recognition that I received when I was in that talent show. So realizing that this yearning for affirmation began when I was a child, the question becomes, How is this tied into the development of my dark side traits of narcissism and compulsiveness?

When I found out that my primary dark side trait was narcissism, I was a bit surprised. I think of narcissists as being self-centered and arrogant, and I didn't see myself as that way at all. I also thought this trait was about making everyone else do whatever I said, and I didn't think that was me either. I later came to realize that my insecurity about not being a good athlete and the affirmation that I sought by being on stage through music and theater was what developed my narcissism. In *Overcoming the Dark Side of Leadership*, McIntosh and Rima say that "narcissistic leaders have an overinflated sense of their importance to the organization and an exhibitionistic need for constant attention and admiration from others, especially those they lead and any person or group to whom they report."[3] When I read that, I thought it fit.

My childhood experiences contributed to my needing constant attention through seeking affirmation after preaching, wanting staff to do what I told them just because I told them, and needing affirmation from other African-American pastors in the Twin Cities. I realized in reflecting on my childhood in this way that even after I became a Christian in high school, this didn't have an impact on my pursuit of acceptance and affirmation by being on stage, and it didn't change after I accepted the call into ministry either. Preaching just became the next stage. I went from seeking affirmation from singing in a talent show, to seeking it on stage as a theater major in college, and then seeking it as a preacher behind a pulpit. Before discovering my primary dark side trait, I didn't understand that in preaching, I had dual and conflicting motives: I wanted to be used by God to preach a word that would lead to transformed lives, but I also wanted to be told that I did a great job. I wanted every sermon to be amazing.

My secondary dark side trait is that of being compulsive. McIntosh and Rima wrote that "the compulsive leader pursues perfection to an extreme, both in personal and organizational life. . . . They continually look for the reassurance and approval of authority figures and are anxious when unsure of their performance and stand-ing."[4] In school, I found myself needing to be called on by the teacher to answer a question, and if I was passed over for another student, I was disappointed. It was as if not being called on or being recog-nized by the teacher meant I wasn't in good standing with him or her. In high school and college, I expected to get a lead role in every play or musical I auditioned for, and when I didn't, I felt I had failed. My sophomore year in college, I won the homecoming talent show, and I was elated. The next year, I came in second and wondered what I had done wrong to not win the favor of the judges. This trait can show up in our relationship with God as well. If we pray for some-thing and it doesn't happen, someone who is compulsive will won-der what he or she has done to displease God. And a typical reaction then is, "If I do more to please God, then God will provide what I'm asking for."

Before becoming a church planter, I served as an associate pas-tor and youth pastor. In each case, the affirmation and approval of the senior pastors were important to me. If there were other associ-ate pastors within the congregation, I wanted to feel that I was the favorite. I understand now that this is how my compulsiveness was working itself out. When I became a senior pastor, I sought this kind of approval from the church members or denominational leaders.

Recognizing this dark side and its effect doesn't mean I can't preach on a regular basis or lead a multi-ethnic and missional min-istry. But it could be the reason that ministry leaders don't want to admit and manage their dark side. They may believe that by acknowledging a dark side, they become disqualified for leadership. Actually just the opposite is the case: refusing to deal with your dark side can either disqualify you for leadership or cause you to live as an unhealthy leader.

My identity in Christ is the solution to the management of these dark side traits. By focusing on spiritual health and leadership development, I can come up with a plan to acknowledge my dark side traits and then manage them. I can also develop a leadership plan based on the other assessments so that I can become a more serving and reconciling leader.

Journaling has been one of ways I manage my dark side traits. I write down how I'm feeling and review the ways in which I have interacted with others on a given day or during the week. If I had a conflict with someone, I ask myself how I contributed to the conflict and how that's connected to my dark side traits. If a particular conflict was with someone of another ethnicity, I use my writing to see if I turned an issue into a racial one when it really wasn't that at all. This processing could then lead me to realize that a conflict was really about my dark side traits. This is the toughest part of the journaling process, but it's needed.

A way to manage your dark side is to spend time alone asking yourself, *Am I the cause of the problem?* My ongoing development plan calls for a consistent time for journaling. I also have a couple of mentors and spiritual directors. I lay out with them all of the struggles, conflicts, and stresses that I'm having in order to get their feedback on how my dark side traits may be coming into play. They also provide suggestions for being led by the Holy Spirit rather than by my dark side.

When I was still in Minnesota and processed conflicts I was having with people, the first thing my spiritual leader, Thom Paige, would always ask me is, "Have you forgiven that person yet?" Most of the time I said yes—and most of the time he wasn't convinced. He also asked me what my time alone with God had been like that week. He wanted to know if I had taken a day off. Overworking and making the church our God can create the opportunities for our dark sides to be dominant. What we like to hide about ourselves becomes what everyone sees. The multi-ethnic and missional leader needs mentors and a spiritual director for accountability in addressing our emotional and spiritual health.

Servant Leadership Development:
Network Servant Profile

In the fall of 2008, we celebrated the fifth-year anniversary as the Sanctuary Covenant Church. A major part of the celebration was a Covenant membership renewal event, which took place the first weekend of October and gave us the opportunity to look again at our vision, purpose, mission, and core values. By doing so, we also gave members the opportunity to renew their membership as well as recommit to serving in ministry. On Saturday of that weekend, we brought in church consultant and speaker Bruce Bugbee. Bugbee and Don Cousins, both former staff members of Willow Creek Church in South Barrington, Illinois, developed a church ministry resource they called Network. Network Ministries International "was established in 1993 to serve and support the ministry and mission of the local church in effective and efficient use of God's people for the kingdom purposes. Building up believers, equipping leaders, and establishing harmonious systems mark the impact of Network Ministries International."[5]

The Network Servant Profile is intended to assist churches in helping their congregants discover their spiritual gifts, personal style, and God-given passion for serving in the body of Christ. Bugbee believes that "healthy churches are functioning on the basis of gift-based ministry teams. They have systems in place for personal discovery and ministry connection."[6]

He preached within a couple of general sessions and led a workshop on the importance of understanding our own kingdom fit. As I listened to him, I couldn't help but reflect on how not managing my dark side or living in my gifts had led me to feel burned out. I talked with the other pastors at the Sanctuary about bringing him back to play a role in our holistic staff development initiative. He returned in early December that year to lead a retreat for our staff, elders, and volunteer ministry team leaders.

When I first thought about this Beloved Life and Leadership Project, I was thinking mainly that it would be a good idea to include spiritual gifts within a holistic approach to staff development. The Servant Profile that comes out of the Network curriculum takes a holistic approach of its own by looking at spiritual gifts, personal style, and ministry passion. This profile then helps us understand where we best fit in advancing God's kingdom. By going through this exercise in our community as staff, elders, and ministry team leaders, we not only would learn more about our individual kingdom purpose, but would see the importance of working together as the local body of Christ.

Knowing my primary dark side trait of narcissism, I needed to go through a process of not just focusing on myself but honoring the kingdom-advancing call of others as well. The Servant Profile is based not just on my reflections but also on feedback from three other people in the church who worked closely with me. We identified my spiritual gifts, in this order:

- Creative communication
- Teaching
- Apostleship/leader

This made sense in connection with my Insights Profile of motivating inspirer. The major way that I motivate and inspire is through preaching and teaching. I also learned that the spiritual gift of apostle/leader showed that, yes, I am a leader, but it's important to understand what kind of leader I am.

This first part of the Servant Profile allowed me to take some time to understand why acknowledging and managing my dark side of narcissism and being compulsive is so important. For example, knowing that one of my spiritual gifts is preaching, I don't need to keep seeking affirmation about my ability to preach well. Also I need to realize that my identity ultimately is not in my spiritual gifts but in my identity in Christ. Resting in this fact is crucial in order to be able to receive constructive criticism of my preaching. Knowing that I have the spiritual gift of apostleship also shows that my approach to leadership ought to be on overseeing and coaching. Again, this fits well with my Insights Profile of being a motivating inspirer. The management of my dark side begins with these questions: When people are around me, are they equipped by being motivated, or are they being limited by my narcissism? Am I focused on people, or are they being forced to focus on me in an unhealthy way? My identity in Christ must drive me back to the understanding that I am God's beloved.

My personal style within the Servant Profile is "people unstructured." This means that I tend to be very conversational, relate well with others, and like being involved in a variety of activities. As I reflected on this, I realized my need to have fun by living in my identity in Christ, using my gifts, and spending time with others. I love fellowship, spontaneity, and connecting.

At the Sanctuary, I particularly liked staff development and fun days. Some people don't believe that a staff having fun together is a good use of resources. But in a multi-ethnic and missional ministry, it's vital. Creating opportunities for play helps to dismantle a culture driven by power.

Recently I planned a staff development day for those I work with now in the Pacific Southwest Region of the Evangelical Covenant church. I wanted it to be both fun and fruitful. We went to a movie, *The Help*. This movie, which focuses on African-American domestics in the Deep South during the civil rights era, helped to develop our cross-cultural awareness and competencies. Before the movie, we went to the House of Chicken and Waffles and had southern soul food. Though we planned this meal, I we didn't have any agenda during the meal. We simply were together, eating, enjoying the fellowship, and learning more about the blessing of being part of a multi-ethnic staff. The unstructured gathering of a multi-ethnic team gives room for the Holy Spirit to do some amazing things. Another way at getting at this would be to have an annual staff retreat. Don't feel the need to plan out every part of the retreat, but do build in some time for fun and fellowship. This can help to build multi-ethnic chemistry with a staff.

I also found that this part of me was helpful in conflict resolution. Because I like being with people, I have the patience and endurance to spend enough time to find out what is at the core of a conflict and work toward reconciliation and healing. I could allow my dark side to cause conflicts or invest time into healing conflicts by living into how God has wired me.

Finally, my Servant Profile revealed my passion for the ministry area of celebration. This meant that my gifts naturally point toward elements within the corporate experience of worship such as preaching, leading the worship, and performing the sacraments. I enjoy working with a team of people doing long-range planning around sermon series, broader themes, and using other elements of the creative arts.

This was not a big revelation to me, but it reminded me that part of my burnout was about my spending a lot of time outside my giftedness. Because I wanted to prove that I was a strong leader, I was engaging in a great deal of effort trying to be an executive pastor. I can do more administrative and operational duties, but it's not my sweet spot, what I do best and like best. My sweet spot is leading from the position of preaching, vision casting, and mobilizing through inspiration. I also love setting big goals, seeing a plan designed to implement those goals, and then celebrating like crazy the transformative results.

It's important for multi-ethnic and missional leaders to know their gifts, use them often, and live in their sweet spot. They should not spend an inordinate amount of time outside their primary giftedness and sweet spot. This realization for me played a role in our eventually hiring an associate pastor of operations. It also meant delegating more leadership responsibilities to the other associate pastors who had been on staff as well.

In living more deeply into my sweet spot for ministry, I had to be willing to empower others on the team to lead. The multi-ethnic leadership team that was collectively living in their giftedness led to greater ministry fruit. We were able to launch more initiatives and reach more people. Under this model, paid staff began to empower volunteer leaders as well, thereby creating a broader culture of a multi-ethnic team leadership. I was less likely to burn out because the weight of the church was not all on my shoulders. Understanding my Servant Profile in connection with the Insights Profile led me to spend time in prayer around identity, gifts, and focusing more on equipping others.

Crossing Cultures: Intercultural Development Inventory

We chose the Intercultural Development tool to look at cross-cultural competencies both in terms of strengths and growth areas. The Intercultural Development Inventory (IDI) is an empirical measure of intercultural sensitivity as conceptualized by Mitchell Hammer and Milton Bennett's Developmental Model of Intercultural Sensitivity.[7] This assessment tool is based on a continuum that begins with ethnocentrism and moves to what Bennett calls ethnorelativism. He also places six experiences across this continuum:

- Denial: Not seeing race and ethnicity as issues at all
- Defense: The state in which one's own race and ethnicity is experienced as the only good one
- Minimization: Working to minimize race and ethnicity as issues

- Acceptance: Recognizing issues of race and ethnicity and the need to work toward unity, harmony, and reconciliation
- Adaptation: The ability to exercise one's cross-cultural awareness
- Integration: The ability to lead in efforts of unity, harmony, and reconciliation and thereby live in a healthy, multi-ethnic, and missional community

As a whole, our staff landed right in the middle of the continuum, minimization, but how we landed there is interesting. Most of the European-Americans on our staff landed in the defense area and the rest of us in the acceptance area, so it was sort of an averaging process. To a degree, I wasn't surprised by this, but it revealed for me how I needed to manage my dark side traits in order to play a reconciling role as a servant leader within this reality. I was still somewhat surprised by the European-Americans' profile because they were working in an intentionally multi-ethnic environment and seemed to enjoy that. Yes, we had tensions at times, but I thought they would be further along the continuum than that. Our facilitator, Dan Jass, a professor at Bethel University, explained that the European-American staff wanted to believe in their hearts that they were further along than they were, which led to defense when conflict arose. Knowing this led me to reflect on how the dark side traits of narcissism and compulsiveness could keep me from being a truth-telling and reconciling leader if I did not manage them well. Because I like being liked and want to be the good guy among the entire staff, I wasn't always willing to risk confronting European-American staff in a healthy way about growth areas that I was seeing around issues of race.

This focus on being truth telling and reconciling while acknowledging my dark side is important because it makes sense of my growth areas within my IDI Profile. The IDI is broken down into subprofiles: intercultural sensitivity, worldview profile, and developmental issues. These subprofiles run a continuum of unresolved, in transition, and resolved. In terms of my individual profile, I was right on the borderline between acceptance and adaptation. But even in light of this, I was unresolved in a couple of areas within the subprofile of developmental issues. One of the areas where I was unresolved was based on my tendency to apply my own cultural values to other cultures, which can lead to thinking that other ethnic groups should be able to navigate ethnic and racial issues in the same way as I do. Instead of understanding the unique stories and perspectives of Asian-Americans, Native Americans, and Hispanics, I could tend to make the African-American story and perspective the one for all ethnic groups, which can lead to other groups' feeling marginalized. So instead of creating a post-Black and post-White church, I might create a church in Black and White.

The other area where I am unresolved is a tendency to shift perspective and behavior according to cultural context. If I'm in a setting with mostly other Blacks, I can behave one way, but if most of the others are White, I could tend to behave another way. This is not all bad, because it is important to be able to communicate well in various cultural contexts. I was specifically unresolved in the area of cognitive frame shifting. For me, this meant that I had a particular mind-set that had been developed over time about how to interact with White people. This was shaped around being in multiple situations where Whites were the dominant group or the authority figure. This was the cognitive framework operating in me.

Once I became the senior pastor of a multi-ethnic church with a significant population of Whites, I was in a position of authority over a group that I had mainly been under the authority of. So although I was the leader, I had to watch out for a default button within myself to back down from healthy leadership if Whites weren't seeming to buy in right away. There were times when I worked to make sure that European-Americans were comfortable in a multi-ethnic environment, but I wasn't working so hard to help non-Whites feel as comfortable. This also points to how I had been socialized in a race-based society where a lot of my upbringing felt as if I was performing for or seeking the approval of European-Americans. For example, as I was growing up, the majority of my teachers were European-American.

During my freshman year at a predominantly European-American university, I needed to feel that the majority students accepted me. It is part of my need for affirmation; I would be more hurt when a European-American had a problem with one of my sermons than one of the Black worshippers did. This revelation about myself through the IDI Profile led me to reflect more deeply on why I'm more affected by conflict with European-Americans than I am with other people groups.

I could see a dual dynamic at play here. In the church, I was working hard to make sure the European-Americans accepted me. These experiences, I now realize, were developing my dark side traits further, which I wasn't even acknowledging at the time. I went into the planting of a multi-ethnic church, which started out 75 percent European-American, not acknowledging this. All of a sudden I could see why I was experiencing burnout: it takes a great deal of energy to suppress awareness of your dark side and work so strenuously at shifting cultural context.

The second part of the dynamic was my not wanting to be seen as a sellout to my own ethnic group as I navigated the waters of trying to live the reconciling life. As I was leading a church that began as majority European-American, I still wanted affirmation from my African-American peers. This was built into me during childhood when I wanted the affirmation of my White teachers during the day at school and my Black parents when I was home in the evening. This is part of my dark side development. It is not my teachers' or parents' fault, but it's the reality of what shapes growing up in a race-based society.

This is why a spiritual health and leadership development plan is so important. If I'm to acknowledge and manage my dark side traits and be a reconciling leader, I must live in the identity of who I am in Christ. By finding my identity in Christ as God's beloved, I no longer had to live for the affirmation and approval of European-Americans in my church or African-American pastors in the surrounding community. My affirmation ultimately comes from knowing that I'm loved by my heavenly Father.

Conclusion

Healthy leadership is important for the development and sustaining of a post-Black and post-White church. This is true of any ministry setting, but especially so because of the unique challenges of leading a multi-ethnic and missional church. Healthy leadership begins with being willing to acknowledge dark side traits as well as how God has uniquely created us for leadership. We must understand that our dark side is managed through living as God's beloved. Multi-ethnic and missional ministry ought to come out of the overflow of intimacy with God, identity in Christ, and the indwelling of the Holy Spirit. Knowing that I'm ultimately loved and affirmed by God as his beloved child is the true empowerment I need, so that I'm not seeking this from people around me in ministry.

We must also remember that we aren't meant to lead in isolation. A team approach to leadership is biblical, as we see in the model of Jesus and the disciples, but it's also important in the post-Black and post-White church. Reconciliation and unity are modeled through ministry teams that work together, support one another, and are strong where the other is weak. In this way we truly function as the body of Christ.

Beloved leadership is a journey, and I continue to experience the joys and the challenges of what it means to be healthy in multi-ethnic and missional ministry. This commitment is about dedicating oneself to a countercultural form of servant leadership. Here are some ideas for living into beloved leadership:

- A monthly day alone with God
- Consistent journaling
- Taking a consistent day off
- A spiritual director and mentors
- Assessment tools that look at personality, gifts, growth areas, and cross-cultural competencies
- A team approach to leadership

9

starting, shifting, and sustaining

I n many biblical stories, God approaches a man or woman with what seems to be a very dangerous or impossible task. God led a boy named David to take on a giant who placed fear in a king and his army. He called Moses to lead a whole people out of slavery in Egypt. He called Queen Esther to confront the king over an unjust decision, putting her own life at risk in the process. These are just a few examples of the challenging calls that come from God within scripture.

The call to develop and lead a post-Black and post-White church today can feel just as challenging. I conclude this book by offering some practical insights for the development, health, and sustenance of the multi-ethnic and missional church. I also bring back some of what I've shared throughout this book so that it might be applied whether you're planting a new church or revitalizing an existing one. I hope that you'll be inspired, motivated, and equipped for this important work.

The Significance of Life Experiences

I don't believe that God calls us to something that he hasn't been preparing us for all along our life experiences. You probably have life experiences that God can use now for the development of a multi-ethnic and missional church. At the time that you were going through these experiences, you may not have felt that they could be used in a significant way for ministry. But by spending intentional time alone with God, you can recall these experiences and use them to fuel the vision for the task God has for you now. I can look back and see how a number of life experiences were working together to prepare me for my ministry calling today.

As I've shared in earlier chapters, I grew up in a Black Baptist church but was also actively involved in a youth group in a predominantly White United Methodist church. The youth group of this church, however, was multi-ethnic and eventually influenced the whole church to become multi-ethnic. My experience in the youth group, coupled with books I read by John Perkins on reconciliation and Christian community development, planted the seed for my passion for the post-Black and post-White church. Being part of a multi-ethnic youth ministry caused me to question why most adults didn't desire to experience church as we knew it as youth each week.

From that multi-ethnic youth group experience, I went on to a predominantly White college. At first, this culture shock caused me great distress, but a sociology class led me to engage more deeply with issues of ethnicity and race. During this time, I also became intrigued with the writings of Martin Luther King Jr. Although he grew up in and became the pastor of a Black church, he led a massive multicultural movement. I became convinced through his writings that if he were still alive, he would have eventually become the pastor of a multiracial church. This belief supplied the thesis statement of my final paper for my master's degree in theology. In his most famous speech, King speaks of a dream where race would cease to be the defining factor of how human beings relate to one another in a diverse society.

I didn't understand why the church couldn't be the living example of that dream on Sunday morning and throughout the week. For eleven years after graduating from college, I served as a youth pastor in various local churches, Black and White, urban and suburban, and in parachurch ministries. By 2001, I was on the staff of the United Methodist church, where I served as an associate pastor overseeing youth and outreach ministries through the church's youth and family foundation, which encompassed a health clinic, legal clinic, transitional housing program, and computer-learning center.

Through these experiences, I couldn't shake my passion for a church that would be a sneak preview of heaven. In 2002, God opened the door for me to connect with the Evangelical Covenant denomination in order to plant the church of my dreams, the church that had been burning in me since high school. My vision was for a church that would be intentionally evangelical, urban, multi-ethnic, and holistic. The holistic part of the vision was the carryover of my experience leading the youth and family foundation. This led to my development into being a missional leader. I went into the venture of church planting believing that the church needed to be both multi-ethnic and missional in order to have credibility in an increasingly multi-ethnic, multicultural, and urbanized reality. Each of these experiences served as a building block for my passion for the post-Black, post-White church. They also were working together to develop my leadership abilities in the areas of vision casting and strategic planning.

Through the Evangelical Covenant church, I have had the opportunity to move vision to reality. The beginning of the pursuit of the vision was a series of meetings to develop an initial diverse core team that would share the vision with me. It's important to realize that God's mission in the world is bigger than just one person. God places experiences in the lives of others and reconciles them to one another in order to live into the vision. We began with a prayerful group of twenty-two, which soon grew to about sixty. As the core team grew, I was further energized by the realization that so many others also had a deep passion for a multi-ethnic and missional church. Some of them had read John Perkins's work as well, some had been part of a multi-ethnic youth ministry, and some had faced difficult challenges in the area of race. Brought together by God and our various life experiences, we began to collectively own the vision of this post-Black, post-White church to be started North Minneapolis.

You may be wondering, "Why Minnesota to plant a multi-ethnic and missional church?" Although most Minnesota residents have primarily a Norwegian or Scandinavian heritage, it is becoming more diverse, especially the Twin Cities of Minneapolis and Saint Paul. Outside of Somalia, for example, Minnesota has the largest Somali population in the world. The Southeast Asian population, mostly Hmong, is growing. Minnesota has a significant Korean-American population, and, interestingly, there are more Korean-American youth in European-American adoptive homes than within Korean-American ones. Minnesota's Latino population is significant as well. Although this diversity mostly shows up in the Twin Cities, it is apparent as well in St. Cloud, Mankato, and Duluth.

North Minneapolis at the time was facing sobering challenges. Schools had been shuttered, housing foreclosures were growing, buildings that had housed community businesses stood empty, and even some churches had forsaken the city for the suburbs.

There was a need for post-Black and post-White churches in the Twin Cities to address not only the diversity of the area but the community challenges as well. What about the area you live in?

What is God calling you and others to do through combining of your life experiences and a new vision for the church?

Planting a post-Black, post-White church begins with visionary leaders who use the empowerment that comes from their own significant life experiences. Starting or shifting an existing church to becoming multi-ethnic and missional begins with a deep unpacking of life experiences and exploring your passion for a specific community. An existing church may need to begin its journey to being multi-ethnic and missional by regaining a passion for the surrounding community. Here is an example of the impact of incorporating life experiences with a passion for a specific community.

Pastor John Fanous is a church planter in the city of Pittsburg in the Bay Area of Northern California. Pittsburg over the years has been affected by the multicultural diversity of nearby cities such as Oakland and San Francisco. Because of this, it has become a multicultural city itself as people who had lived in Oakland or San Francisco made their way out to Pittsburg, in some cases looking for better housing prices and better schools for their children. This made it the perfect place for John and a few others to start a new kind of church. Edgewater Covenant Church exists today as a multi-ethnic and missional church in part because of John's life experiences and the impact they've had on him. John is an American-born Egyptian, but he didn't reflect much on the significance of his ethnicity and its connection to his call to multi-ethnic ministry until he was in college. It was then that his involvement with InterVarsity Christian Fellowship, which lifts up multi-ethnicity as a biblical value, led him to develop a deep hunger for his Middle Eastern heritage.

As John grew in his Christian faith through the study of scripture, he also was growing in his passion for multi-ethnic ministry. He was involved in InterVarsity not only as a student but also as a staff person and assisted in starting campus fellowships for African-Americans, Latinos, and Pacific Islanders. These fellowships included

Bible-centered discussions on race and ethnic identity. Working with such a diversity of people played a major role in leading him to plant Edgewater. This young church of about two hundred congregants is now 50 percent Hispanic, 40 percent European-American, and 10 percent African-American and Asian. When I moved to California, this became my family's home church.

Starting with Purpose

The post-Black and post-White church starts through a vision that comes from the collective life experiences of leaders as they discover their true identity and calling. But the vision must then lead to the development of purpose. Purpose expands who we desire to be into what we are about. Edgewater's purpose is, "Loving God, Loving People, and Serving Our Community." Loving God is connected to a multi-ethnic and creative experience of worship, where love for God can be expressed. Loving people is lived out through multi-ethnic small groups with a focus on discipleship. These groups are encouraged not just to meet together for prayer, Bible study, and fellowship, but also to go out into the community of Pittsburg and serve. A lot of their service is focused around Stoneman Elementary School, where the church currently worships. Members donate school and office supplies, sponsor needy families, and run summer day camps for children in the community.

Developing a purpose statement was also important in starting the Sanctuary Covenant Church. We began with this one: "To change the face of the church by reconciling the people of the city to God and one another."

In a society where race is an issue, there is a need for a reconciling community that finds its identity in being the beloved church. If the love of God through Jesus Christ is powerful enough to bring about salvation, then surely it's powerful enough to deal with the dividing wall of race in our society. Since its inception, the Sanctuary has been a post-Black, post-White church. This began by intentionally building a multi-ethnic core team, which then led to a multi-ethnic elder board, experience of corporate worship, and then staff. From there we worked to move toward becoming a missional church through community engagement. Our goal was to become a healthy and self-sustaining church. Later our goal was to create a movement for developing other post-Black, post-White churches.

Our ability to become a missional church showed up in the development of our core values and the creation of the Sanctuary Community Development Corporation (CDC), which enabled the church to address some of the disparities within the surrounding community. Initially the CDC focused on economic and youth development through after-school programs and a job readiness initiative. The core values, which assisted us in the intentional development of working toward a multi-ethnic, missional, and reconciling community, became known as the 5 Es (evangelism, engagement, experience, equipping, and empowerment), and the ministry areas of the church were created from them. These 5 Es are all rooted intentionally around being multi-ethnic and missional and can be used in multi-ethnic church planting or revitalization.

The post-Black and post-White church must be grounded in scripture and in values, from which ministry models can developed for the long-term sustaining of the ministry. Scripture is important so that the post-Black and post-White church is not seen primarily as a social experiment or a move of political correctness. Within evangelicalism, of which I'm a part, biblical foundation provides the history of seeing multi-ethnicity, multiculturalism, and social justice as theologically liberal.

How to Use the Core Values

Developing the biblical mandate for the post-Black and post-White church is the beginning. Next is dealing with the implications of what the scripture is saying to us today. Core values give clarity to how the scriptural implications will be expressed in a real multi-ethnic and missional community.

Evangelism and Outreach

This is where the missional side of the church is developed. In order for the church to advance the kingdom of God today, it must connect evangelism with ministries of compassion, mercy, and justice. Kingdom advancement must include opportunities to know Jesus Christ as Lord and Savior, Liberator, and the Giver of purpose. Throughout the gospels, we see examples of Jesus's impact on the whole person. In Matthew 9, for example, alone, Jesus forgave sins, restored a paralyzed person to mobility, healed a diseased woman, and brought a dead girl back to life. The chapter concludes with Jesus looking with compassion on the diverse multitude of people he was engaging for the kingdom. It is the love of God embodied in his Son that leads to salvation, healing, and holistic transformation. This is a missional blueprint for the post-Black, post-White church.

For this holistic approach to evangelism to be possible, the church must be equipped to deal with the issues, challenges, and barriers of its surrounding community in some meaningful way. Again in Matthew 9, we are told that Jesus went from town to town, proclaiming the kingdom, healing the sick, and casting out evil spirits. At the beginning of Matthew 10, he empowered his followers to do the same. The multi-ethnic and missional church must take the same approach empowered by the Holy Spirit in its own community.

In planting the Sanctuary Covenant Church, we had a desire to see people in North Minneapolis come to Christ and discover their life purpose in God as well. Many people within the community were in search of experiencing life differently and having a greater sense of purpose. It may be too that those who are behaving in a way that hurts their community don't have a sense of their life purpose.

Discovering life purpose means nothing to those who are not equipped and empowered to live out that purpose. If someone has a strong sense of purpose but doesn't know Jesus as Lord and Savior, ultimately what difference does that sense of purpose make? At the same time, if someone knows Jesus as Lord and Savior but is not able to graduate from high school and go on from there to live out God's purpose for their lives, what difference does that make? Knowing God and living out God's purpose for life is the journey of discipleship through evangelism and outreach. A missional church should not just be focused on leading people toward becoming empowered and purposed disciples.

This approach to evangelism and outreach is dependent on a love for people cross-culturally. Pastor John Teter leads Fountain of Life Covenant church in Long Beach, California. Because I've already talked about one John, I will simply call him "Teter." Like Pastor John Fanous, he too has a background with InterVarsity Christian Fellowship. He served on the staff of its campus ministry at the University of Southern California. Now, along with leading a multi-ethnic and missional church in Southern California, he also is the National Evangelism leader for the Evangelical Covenant church. Teter has a tremendous passion for taking a long-term, relational approach to evangelism that includes equipping people to invest in relationships cross-culturally.

I've had the opportunity to hang out with Teter on a few occasions either in or close by his community, and every time we run into many people of various ethnic backgrounds who know him. They are not all Christians. He just has a passion to build relationships with people cross-culturally. He has shared Christ with people this way, found new staff, and gained much credibility in his community. After attending one of the experiences of worship at Fountain of Life, I had lunch with some of the staff and other key leaders. Many of them had stories of meeting Teter in various settings within the community and then eventually finding their way to the church. One young lady was a lifeguard at the pool where Teter was swimming one afternoon. She is now a leader in the youth ministry.

There is no question that his approach to evangelism comes out of a great love for a multicultural world. You can't start a multi-ethnic and missional church if you see the multicultural world around you as the enemy. Some churches don't engage the diverse world because instead of seeing God in that world, they see a culture of evil. It's not that there isn't evil in the world, but God in the world trumps evil in the world. Jesus prays in the Gospel of John in a way that defines our role as ministry leaders in the world: "I do not ask Thee to take them out of the world, but to keep them from the evil one. They are not of the world, even as I am not of the world. Sanctify them in the truth; Thy word is truth. As Thou didst send Me into the world, I also have sent them into the world" (John 17:15–18).

Jesus prayed that his disciples would be in the world as he was. He was sent into a diverse but broken world because of God's love for it in order to bring about reconciliation and redemption. We are to be in that world as an extension of God's love. This should be the hope we live by as we engage this world. You can't live this way if you see terms like diversity, multi-ethnicity, and multicultural as simply secular, worldly, and somehow evil. Teter passionately lives within this reality of loving people, and he has seen the lives of students, businesspeople, and gang members transformed through the ministries of Fountain of Life Covenant church. Teter also has a heart for community development and transformation. This has led to the church starting a family center that provides a holistic approach to missional work.

Engagement and Care

Ultimately for the church to be a beloved and reconciling community, it must be a place where we engage in each other's lives. The name of the church we planted in North Minneapolis was significant. *Sanctuary* refers to a dwelling place, a safe haven for people to come to. But it also refers to something much more. We found a biblical foundation for this in Ezekiel 37: "And I will make a covenant of peace with them; it will be an everlasting covenant with them. And I will place them and multiply them, and will set My sanctuary in their midst forever. My dwelling place will also be with them; and I will be their God, and they will be My people" (Ezekiel 37:26–27).

The sanctuary that God provides is not just something that you go into but also something that God puts on us. As we engage in life together cross-culturally, we experience sanctuary. It was actually my wife, Donecia, who named the church that we planted together. She had a desire to be part of the development of a community where there were authentic and deepening relationships between people who wouldn't normally go to church. Her life experiences not only instilled in her a passion for a diverse church; she also had a heart for those she had gone to high school and college with who were having a hard time finding community through the church. They were visiting churches but in some cases not finding the experience of sanctuary. Sanctuary ultimately is not a place, but a people covered by the reconciling Spirit of God. When we began the Sanctuary, we wanted its name to point to a desire to be a beloved church and a reconciling community. We hoped it would be a beloved and reconciling community by caring for one another and bearing each other's burdens. But how do people truly care for one another if they haven't been in authentic relationships with others across racial and ethnic boundaries?

You have to be intentional about getting people together in authentic relationships across racial lines. Potluck meals were important for us in our early development. When we were just a core team of fewer than a hundred people, we had potluck meals where we asked people to bring a dish to share that represented their culture or upbringing. During this multi-ethnic buffet, I would lead a Bible study centered on themes for multi-ethnic and missional church development.

Creating spaces for fellowship supported by strong hospitality is important in multi-ethnic ministry. There is something powerful about walking into a room and being greeted by people of different ethnicities, all with smiling faces. What eventually became our community groups grew out of intentional, diverse fellowship events, prayer gatherings, and Bible studies. As relationships developed, the blessings of being reconciled to one another began to take place. People began to bear one another's burdens. They were caring for one another and meeting each other's needs, and race was no longer a barrier to these beloved acts taking place. It wasn't that race was not an issue, but it wasn't blocking God's love flowing through us to care for each other.

Experience of Worship

A multi-ethnic experience of worship seeks to provide a sneak preview of heaven. Why not practice here on earth the ways in which we will worship in eternity? Why not do it as often as we can? I believe that those outside church who experience diversity everywhere else they go in society except the church probably use that as part of their excuse for not going. For the younger generation especially, a segregated church just doesn't make sense.

In planting the Sanctuary, we wanted to be intentional about engaging the multi-ethnic realities of our surrounding community and world through our experience of corporate worship. Although I served primarily as the preacher within the experience of worship, I approached worship each Sunday as an artist, a holder of a bachelor's degree in theater arts, and a member of the hip-hop generation. From this background, I saw it as important to use as many artistic elements as possible to proclaim the kingdom of God and project the beloved community. The experience of worship was the primary way to share our unique cultural gifts with one another to the glory of God.

The House Covenant church in Chicago, led by Phil Jackson, offers another example of a hip-hop church and how it operates. To reach the unchurched in the community on Chicago's West Side, worship services are held on Saturday nights. Pastor Phil, as most people call him, usually preaches in a T-shirt, jeans, and sneakers. Hip-hop artists lead the congregation in praise and worship with tracks filled with loud bass coming out of multiple speakers. This church's worship services are not for everyone, but they are reaching an emerging urban and multi-ethnic generation that feels unwelcomed by many traditional Black and White churches.

Equipping and Formation

The beloved Christ-centered, multi-ethnic, and reconciling community cannot just be a cool organic worship experience; it must shape our being and daily living as Christians. We are called to be reconcilers in the world, and in order to grow as a post-Black, post-White church movement, we must focus on discipleship and formation. This is about strategically discipling in a way that raises up reconcilers and laborers (that is, those who are committed to serving for the advancement of God's kingdom). To address this, you have to provide biblically based classes focusing on issues of the local community, race, justice, and reconciliation. At the Sanctuary, we eventually provided retreats for men, women, married couples, singles, and young adults. Even those who became members of the Sanctuary and had grown up in church and were already Christian were in need of a reframing of Christianity and what being a disciple means. The reason is that most of them had grown up in segregated churches and brought with them a Black or White Christianity.

This area of our ministry was the hardest because many had a tough time admitting that they needed a new Christian formation. This value probably should have been called "equipping and re-formation" instead of "equipping and formation." Being part of a multi-ethnic and missional church can be like a second conversion of sorts. This is where discipleship is about equipping people to live into the third culture that Dave Gibbons talks about, that is, the development of kingdom culture or beloved community. In New Song Church in Irvine, California, where Gibbons is pastor, developing third culture has become the way in which this congregation has provided a model for being post-Black and post-White. The church is mostly made up of various Asian-American groups, but there are strong representations as well of European-Americans, African-Americans, and Hispanics.

Third culture is the ethos that those in this church hope their discipleship focus will create. This beloved community is realized through a way of finding new identity in Christ. Instead of new identity being about changing behavior alone, it's a rethinking of race. What does it mean as a Christian to find your identity not in the man-made social structure of race but in being a citizen of the beloved community of God? Equipping and formation in this context is about relearning. In the post-Black and post-White church, members must be humble enough to relearn church and what it means to be a disciple in order to reengage a multicultural world. This is the part of the multi-ethnic and missional church that is the most challenging and why some don't stay for the long haul. It's difficult to let go of belief systems forged in childhood. Some people are okay with sitting next to someone of a different ethnicity every Sunday but aren't as interested in having their sense of what it means to be a follower of Christ challenged. As difficult as it may be, though, this work of relearning is of utmost importance. It also sets up the process of sending members back into a multicultural world for missional purposes.

Empowerment and Advancement

The Sanctuary today is about empowering people to advance the kingdom of God in the world around them. There is a great multi-ethnic and multicultural mission field outside every American's front door, but some will not take advantage of it because they feel ill equipped. Some attempt to engage it, but struggle because they're ultimately bringing a White or Black gospel into a multicultural reality. Discipleship and formation ought to tie into a focus on what Kingdom Building Ministries, an evangelism and missional development ministry in the Denver, Colorado, area, refers to as "labor-ship." There is a need for laborers, but those laborers must understand that they are ultimately empowered by a new view of Jesus and by the Holy Spirit. If this isn't realized and used, it could limit what the Spirit desires within a person. Kingdom advancement is about the indwelling of the Holy Spirit, understanding our gifts and calling, and combining that with a holistic and multi-ethnic understanding of the gospel. This is why a relearning of who Jesus is for many is so important. Christ is now in us through the Holy Spirit, but our imagery of Jesus is important for our empowerment. I realize that ultimately the Holy Spirit is an invisible force within us, but there is a connection to how we visualize and imagine Jesus. There is a connection because God the Father, Jesus, and the Holy Spirit make up the full essence of God, or what we call the Trinity. But the reality is also that how we view Jesus influences how we are led by the Holy Spirit as we engage the world around us. If we imagine Jesus as White, for example, we can be led by the Holy Spirit in one way. If we imagine Jesus as Black, we can be led another way. If we imagine Jesus as liberal, we're led still another way. When we can imagine the authentic multi-ethnic Jesus, who transcends conservative and liberal, Black and White, we are empowered to advance the kingdom of God in new ways.

Empowerment is also about discovering your own natural and spiritual gifts. It's about seeing the combination of these gifts and your unique cultural experiences as God-glorifying opportunities. Advancement is about using those gifts and cultural experiences to proclaim the kingdom of God for life and community transformation. This value lifts up the priesthood of all believers that everyone has been gifted by God to make a kingdom difference in an ever-increasing multi-ethnic and multicultural world. God not only mandates us to make disciples of all nations; he empowers us to live out this mandate by advancing his kingdom in the world.

Let's Go

The multi-ethnic and missional church is a relatively small but growing movement. Although the world around us demands this kind of church, multi-ethnic ministry continues to be marginalized. We are seeing more and more missional conversations and resources, but still rarely find these in the area of multi-ethnic ministry. If this doesn't change, the church will find itself in a much deeper crisis.

Leaders with a passion for multi-ethnic and missional ministry cannot afford to wait until this kind of ministry becomes mainstream. The time is now. Though we go into this work in many cases underresourced and feeling unqualified, we must go nevertheless. We must find like-minded people being led by the Spirit to start and strengthen churches to look like the kingdom of God, where we will live eternally. We can realize a post-Black and post-White church today and play a role in expanding a movement that strengthens the church into the future.

notes

Introduction: Enter the Sanctuary

1. I served as the founding and senior pastor of the Sanctuary Covenant Church from 2003 to 2010. In April 2010, I was elected superintendent of the Pacific Southwest Conference of the Evangelical Covenant church.

2. All biblical quotations in this book are from the New American Standard Bible.

3. I have been asked by some evangelical and European-American Christians why I use hyphenated descriptions of groups of people: African-American and European-American, for example. First, race is unbiblical. It is not part of the way in which God created humankind. Race is a man-made social structure with no strong biological grounding. In scripture, people are mentioned by tribes, nationalities, and ethnicities but not by racial groups. Second, I believe that it is possible to live as a U.S. citizen and still honor your immigrant or, in my case, African and slave past. I don't glorify my slave past, but I honor those who suffered, died, and provided free labor during an oppressive and horrifying part of our American history. The life I live today is lived on the shoulders of my ancestors who were slaves. Being able to connect to those in my past as well as live as an American citizen are to me part of what makes this country special. I know that not everyone will agree with me. They say that we are all Americans and that all the hyphens should be done away with. I understand their position, but I respectfully disagree. A third reason that I recognize myself as African-American stems from an experience on my first trip to Africa, described in Chapter Three, when the group waiting for us at the airport proclaimed, "Welcome home!"

4. C. P. DeYoung, M. O. Emerson, G. Yancey, and K. Chai Kim, *United by Faith: The Multiracial Congregation as an Answer to the Problem of Race* (New York: Oxford University Press, 2003), p. 3.

5. Ibid., p. 2.

Chapter One: Reconciling, Multi-Ethnic, and Missional

1. C. P. DeYoung, *Coming Together in the Twenty-First Century: The Bible's Message in an Age of Diversity* (Valley Forge, Pa.: Judson Press, 2009), p. 61.

2. M. DeYmaz, *Building a Healthy Multi-Ethnic Church: Mandate, Commitments, and Practices of a Diverse Congregation* (San Francisco: Jossey-Bass, 2007), p. xxix.

3. J. M. Washington, *A Testament of Hope: The Essential Writings and Speeches of Martin Luther King, Jr.* (San Francisco: HarperCollins, 1986), pp. 107–109.

4. P. Jenkins, *The Next Christendom: The Coming of Global Christianity* (New York: Oxford University Press, 2002), p. 2.

5. I mostly use the term *post-Black, post-White church* to define one that is multi-ethnic and missional. Sometimes, in an attempt to make a deeper theological case for presenting this kind of church as the best model for kingdom advancement, I use the terms the *beloved church* or the *beloved community*. I unpack the beloved church more deeply in my previous book, *Jump: Into a Life of Further and Higher* (Colorado Springs: David C. Cook, 2010).

6. K. L. Edwards, *The Elusive Dream: The Power of Race in Interracial Churches* (New York: Oxford University Press, 2008), p. 6.

7. J. Perkins, *With Justice for All: A Strategy for Community Development* (Ventura, Calif.: Regal, 2007), p. 11. The original edition was published in 1981.

8. Ibid., p. 114.

Chapter Two: Moving the Church Beyond Crisis, Captivity, and Comfort

1. D. T. Olson, *The American Church in Crisis* (Grand Rapids, Mich.: Zondervan, 2008), pp. 15–16.

2. Ibid., p. 130.

3. Ibid., p. 152.

4. "Top 50 Cities in the U.S. by Population and Rank," http://www .infoplease.com/ipa/A0763098.html.

5. M. Rosenberg, "Largest Metropolitan Areas: The 30 Largest Metropolitan Areas in the U.S.," About.com Geography, July 22, 2009, http:// geography.about.com/od/lists/a/csa2005.htm.

6. "An Older and More Diverse Nation by Midcentury," U.S. Census Bureau, Aug. 14, 2008.

7. K. R. Humes, N. A. Jones, and R. R. Ramirez, "Overview of Race and Hispanic Origin: 2010," U.S. Census Briefs, Mar. 2011.

8. S. R. Ennis, M. Rios-Vargas, and N. G. Albert, "The Hispanic Population: 2010," U.S. Census Briefs, Mar. 2011.

9. L. Hixson, B. B. Helper, and M. O. Kim, "The White Population: 2010," U.S. Census Briefs, Sept. 2011.

10. S. Rastogi, T. D. Johnson, E. M. Hoeffel, and M. P. Drewery, "The Black Population: 2010," U.S. Census Briefs, Sept. 2011.

11. S.-C. Rah, *The Next Evangelicalism: Freeing the Church from Western Cultural Captivity* (Downers Grove, Ill.: InterVarsity Press, 2009), pp. 21–22.

12. Ibid., p. 30.

13. Ibid., p. 45.

14. Ibid., p. 49.

15. Ibid., p. 72.

Chapter Three: Compassion, Mercy, and Justice

1. I use the term *advancing the kingdom* rather than *sharing the good news* because *good news* has been reduced to meaning solely talking to someone one-on-one about Jesus. I used to go to conferences where teens would be sent out into the streets to witness to people. They were supposed to hand a brochure to someone or sit down and share a few scriptures and then pray the prayer of salvation with them. If this approach was unsuccessful, the teens were basically told, "Don't worry about it; you planted a seed." That may very well be true, but this is not the complete gospel. The good news of the kingdom deals with you in your eternity *and* right now.

Chapter Four: Race

1. Brookings Institution Metropolitan Policy Program, *Mind the Gap: Reducing Disparities to Improve Regional Competitiveness in the Twin Cities* (Washington, D.C.: Brookings Institution Metropolitan Policy Program, 2005).

2. J. Piper, *Bloodlines: Race, Cross, and the Christian* (Wheaton, Ill.: Crossway, 2011), p. 234.

3. J. Barndt, *Dismantling Racism: The Continuing Challenge to White America* (Minneapolis: Augsburg Fortress, 1991), p. 28.

4. George A. Yancey, *Beyond Black and White: Reflections on Racial Reconciliation* (Grand Rapids, Mich.: Baker Books, 1996), p. 18.

5. E. Smith, *Jump: Into a Life of Further and Higher* (Colorado Springs: David C. Cook, 2010).

6. J. D. Hays, *From Every People and Nation: A Biblical Theology of Race* (Downers Grove, Ill.: InterVarsity Press, 2003), p. 55.

7. Evangelical Covenant Church, "Invitation to Racial Reconciliation," http://www.covchurch.org/resources/invitation-to-racial-righteousness/#more-428.

Chapter Five: The Gift of the Black Church

1. A. H. Pinn and A. B. Pinn, *Introduction to Black Church History* (Minneapolis: Fortress Press, 2002), pp. 1–2.

2. Ibid., p. 12.

3. It's interesting to me that European-American evangelicals will talk about underground churches in places such as Asia and eastern European today, but they don't talk about or are seemingly unaware of the Black church's beginnings as an underground church. Christianity was not illegal, but the Black church was.

4. J. Cone, *Black Theology and Black Power* (Maryknoll, N.Y.: Orbis Books, 1997), pp. 5–6.

5. C. F. Ellis Jr., *Free at Last? The Gospel in the African-American Experience*, 2nd ed. (Downers Grove, Ill.: InterVarsity Press 1996), p. 93.

6. Quoted in ibid., p. 140.

7. T. Campolo, "It's Friday, But Sunday's Coming" (sermon preached at the Urbana Conference, University of Illinois, Champaign, Ill., 1978). Video.

8. Darrell L. Guder, professor of evangelism and church growth at Columbia Theological Seminary, describes the missional church as a sending church: "With the term missional we emphasize the essential nature and vocation of the church as God's called and sent people." D. Guder, *Missional Church: A Vision for the Sending of the Church in North America* (Grand Rapids, Mich.: Eerdmans, 1998), p. 1.

9. J. H. Cone, *God of the Oppressed*, rev. ed. (Maryknoll, N.Y.: Orbis Books, 1997), p. 16.

10. Quoted in ibid., p. 19.

11. R. M. Franklin, *Crisis in the Village: Restoring Hope in African-American Communities* (Minneapolis: Fortress Press, 2007), p. 111.

Chapter Six: Creating a Post-White Church

1. K. W. Peterson, "Transforming the Covenant: The Emergence of Ethnic Diversity in a Swedish American Denomination," *Covenant Quarterly,* Feb. 2009.

2. G. P. Anderson (ed.), *Covenant Roots: Sources and Affirmations,* 2nd ed. (Chicago: Covenant Publications, 1999), pp. 1–2.

3. Z. E. Hawkinson, *Anatomy of the Pilgrim Experience: Reflections on Being a Covenanter* (Chicago: Covenant Publications, 2000), pp. 14–15.

4. Hospitality House Youth Development, "Brief History," n.d., http://www .hhyd.org/new/?page_id=9.

5. "The Five-Fold Test," http://www.covchurch.org/resources/files/2011/ 02/2-Five-fold-Test.pdf.

6. G. Yee, "The Unfolding Face of the Covenant," *Covenant Companion,* Sept. 2009, p. 8.

Chapter Seven: Leadership

1. G. L. McIntosh and S. D. Rima Sr., *Overcoming the Dark Side of Leadership: The Paradox of Personal Dysfunction* (Grand Rapids, Mich.: Baker, 1997).

Chapter Eight: The Beloved Life and Leadership Project

1. S. D. Rima, *Rethinking the Successful Church: Finding Serenity in God's Sovereignty* (Grand Rapids, Mich.: Baker, 2002), p. 52.

2. A. Lothian, *Insights* (Dundee, Scotland, 2008).

3. G. L. McIntosh and S. D. Rima Sr., *Overcoming the Dark Side of Leadership: The Paradox of Personal Dysfunction* (Grand Rapids, Mich.: Baker, 1997), p. 98.

4. Ibid., p. 88.

5. B. Bugbee and D. Cousins, *Network Participant's Guide* (Grand Rapids, Mich.: Zondervan, 1994), p. 158.

6. Ibid., p. 15.

7. M. R. Hammer and M. J. Bennett, *The IDI Manual* (Portland, Ore.: Intercultural Communication Institute, 2001).

about the author

Efrem Smith is an internationally recognized preacher. He also consults on issues of multi-ethnicity, leadership, and community development.

Smith served as founding pastor of the Sanctuary Covenant Church and president of the Sanctuary Community Development Corporation in Minneapolis, Minnesota. Currently he is the superintendent of the Pacific Southwest Conference of the Evangelical Covenant church. He is also an itinerant speaker with Kingdom Building Ministries and the author of the books *Raising Up Young Heroes, The Hip-Hop Church,* and *Jump.*

index